T0312199

THE PROCUREMENT MODELS HANDBOOK

Building from the previous two successful editions, *The Procurement Models Handbook* is an essential resource for everyone working in the procurement profession, including those selling directly to it. The authors provide the reader with a useful guide to the business models most frequently applied in the procurement and supply chain arena.

Procurement and supply chain management are two of the highest contributors to corporate success in the modern world. This third edition is a new revised international version with additional tools that reflect the value of procurement in our globally-connected world. The authors have included over 50 well-established strategic and operational models that have a proven track record of delivering value over years of practice. Each model is presented pictorially, with explanatory commentary on its practical application to support.

These models are designed to save unnecessary cost and deliver significant benefits for their user and have been carefully selected by the authors based on their originality and usefulness for practical application in the context of procurement and the supply chain. *The Procurement Models Handbook* is an invaluable and enduring source of reference for practitioners and business managers, as well as an essential learning support for business and procurement students.

Andrea Cordell is a well-known international speaker and author on strategy, negotiation and procurement-related matters. She has worked in senior positions at several global organisations and is currently the managing director of Cordie Ltd, a leading sales and procurement training and consulting company.

Ian Thompson is a leading authority on procurement and category management, having worked in a number of senior positions at global organisations and consulting companies. He is one of the founding directors of Cordie Ltd, a leading sales and procurement training and consulting company.

THE PROCUREMENT MODELS HANDBOOK

Third Edition

Andrea Cordell and Ian Thompson

LONDON AND NEW YORK

Third edition published 2019
by Routledge
2 Park Square, Milton Park, Abingdon, Oxon OX14 4RN

and by Routledge
52 Vanderbilt Avenue, New York, NY 10017

Routledge is an imprint of the Taylor & Francis Group, an informa business

First edition published by Chartered Institute of Purchasing & Supply
Second edition published by Chartered Institute of Purchasing & Supply 2013

British Library Cataloguing-in-Publication Data
A catalogue record for this book is available from the British Library

Library of Congress Cataloging-in-Publication Data
Names: Cordell, Andrea, 1965– author. | Thompson, Ian, 1967– author.
Title: The procurement models handbook / Andrea Cordell and Ian Thompson.
Other titles: Purchasing models handbook
Description: Third edition. | Abingdon, Oxon ; New York, NY : Routledge, 2019. |
Earlier editions published as: Purchasing models handbook: a guide to the
most popular business models used in purchasing / Andrea Reynolds
and Ian Thompson. | Includes bibliographical references and index.
Identifiers: LCCN 2018059900 | ISBN 9780815375616 (hardback) |
ISBN 9780815375609 (pbk.) | ISBN 9781351239509 (ebook)
Subjects: LCSH: Industrial procurement. | Purchasing.
Classification: LCC HD39.5 .C668 2019 | DDC 658.7/2—dc23
LC record available at https://lccn.loc.gov/2018059900

ISBN: 978-0-8153-7561-6 (hbk)
ISBN: 978-0-8153-7560-9 (pbk)
ISBN: 978-1-3512-3950-9 (ebk)

Typeset in Bembo
by Apex CoVantage, LLC

CONTENTS

FIGURES

ACKNOWLEDGEMENTS

This compendium of well-known procurement, supply chain and management models would never have been created without the help and encouragement of others.

In particular, we acknowledge all the diligent students across our five Cordie study centres who have been an inspiration for this book. When we developed the first edition back in 2008, it was with you in mind. So many management models seemed to be 'on repeat' throughout professional qualification syllabuses, we knew this handbook would help to cut through the hyperbole and give you day-to-day practical help. We hope you enjoy!

In addition, since establishing our company back in 2003, we have had the pleasure of meeting tens of thousands of hard-working practitioners throughout the procurement profession. While the professional bodies are trying, we have felt not enough is being done to disseminate knowledge and practical help. As a professional, this should be your right and we hope this handbook offers easy-to-understand practical guidance with your work.

Our final words of gratitude go to the production teams at Cordie and Routledge in helping create this new improved third edition. Thank you.

ABOUT THE AUTHORS

Andrea Cordell is the managing director of Cordie Ltd, a leading sales, procurement and supply-chain knowledge and education company. While she is well known for her enthusiastic and interactive public speaking style, her specialist subject is the human dynamics and hypnotic language surrounding commercial relationships and, in particular, subliminal linguistics.

Andrea has an MBA from Henley Business School and is an NLP Master, as well as being a licensed MBTI® Assessor and a registered EQ Tester. She is a Fellow of both the Institute of Sales and Management (ISM) and the Chartered Institute of Procurement & Supply (CIPS).

Ian Thompson is one of the directors and cofounders of Cordie Ltd, as well as a Fellow of both the Institute of Leadership and Management (ILM) and CIPS. He currently leads commercial training programmes on a worldwide basis, where his specialist subjects include category management, strategic sourcing and public procurement regulation.

Prior to establishing Cordie, Ian led sourcing teams in several large blue-chip organisations and before that worked as a chartered engineer on major infrastructure projects.

Ian has set up five successful CIPS study centres and helped Cordie twice win the United Kingdom's national training awards for 'outstanding training delivery'.

Other books by Andrea and Ian include:

- The Category Management Handbook
- The Negotiation Handbook
- Emotional Intelligence and Negotiation

INTRODUCTION

The development of procurement as a professional management discipline has been a remarkable story over the last four decades. During this time we have witnessed the increased reach and influence of procurement and supply chain management; a so-called 'Cinderella' function that has transformed from a predominantly administrative and clerical discipline through to a valuable and strategic capability in most forward-thinking organisations.

There have been many reasons for this transformation, led perhaps in part by the need for new sources of competitive advantage and innovation and also by the vision and drive of a few notable business leaders and academics.

This book captures that spirit: the quest for continuous improvement, innovation and strategic development. It provides both students and business managers with a simple and effective synthesis of the most influential thinking that has helped develop purchasing today.

The aim of this book is to provide a useful guide of the business models most frequently applied in the procurement and supply chain arena. It is hoped that both students and practitioners alike will find it a valuable and enduring source of reference.

Development of procurement

Several commentators have discussed the remarkable development of procurement. In one of our earlier texts (Reynolds, 2003), we charted the growth of capabilities as shown in Figure 0.1:

What is interesting to note in this model is how procurement has successfully developed from a strong foundation of technical tools and processes, through to more sophisticated and holistic management techniques, finally broadening to the 'softer' skills that require greater finesse and application.

Professors Arjan van Weele and Frank Rozemeijer (1996) have also modelled a development curve for procurement shown in Figure 0.2:

In this model (Figure 0.2), van Weele and Rozemeijer (1996) chart procurement as a function that needs to develop through six classic stages from tactical 'price-based' order placement, through to integrated and value-adding supply chains.

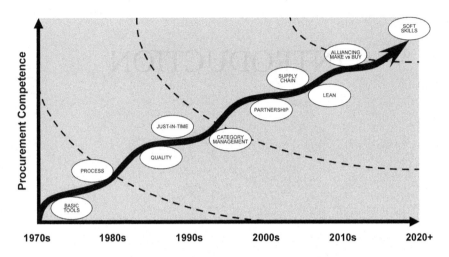

Figure 0.1 Capabilities Growth

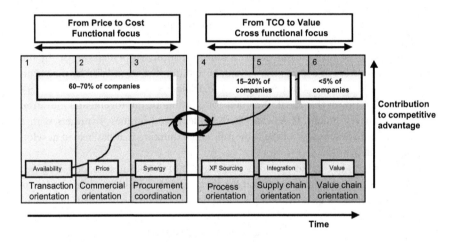

Figure 0.2 Development of Procurement

Source: adapted from van Weele and Rozemeijer (1996).

However the development of procurement is viewed, the fact remains that it has changed – dramatically – and in so doing it has had to develop its sophistication. There are numerous management models that have been innovated, debated, refined and disseminated – each contributing to the body of knowledge that now constitutes the 'profession'. This book presents readers with a summary of just some of the pre-eminent models that are now available.

Choice of models

In preparing this third edition we have reviewed over 200 academic models and business tools, as well as numerous papers, articles and texts.

Picking out the most relevant models is always going to be open to subjectivity and conjecture. However, our selection criteria for the models presented in this text have been:

- Whether they can be applied practically in the context of procurement and the supply chain
- Whether they are generally regarded as being useful in relation to the activities of the modern organisation operating in today's dynamic business environment
- Whether they are an original concept, rather than later adaptations.

The choice is our own; however, we have sought advice from leading procurement academics and practitioners to arrive at a consensus.

Presentation of models

The models are presented so that both a pictorial and explanatory commentary is available to the reader. The format for each is as follows:

- **Overview** – A brief introduction of the model.
- **Elements** – A description or definition of the key parts of the model.
- **So what?** – A guide as to how the model is generally used in a practical sense in the business world.
- **Procurement application** – Suggestions as to how the model can be applied specifically in a procurement and supply chain context.
- **Limitations** – An open and even-handed critique of the model.
- **Further reading** – A pointer to key works and/or text on the underpinning theory that originated the model.
- **Associated models** – A list of models that could potentially be linked or related.

Third edition

We are grateful to Routledge for the production of this third edition of *The Procurement Models Handbook*, not least of all because of their global and independent reach as well as the variety of modern formats with which they can disseminate this important work. The fact that this publication is now in its third edition is testament alone to the fact it fulfils a valuable need in the procurement profession.

We have introduced a number of new models in this edition, as well as revising some from previous editions. Notably we have introduced a couple of new models that are widely used in practice, but yet to be unsupported in the academic literature.

Procurement cannot simply be left to researchers or academics to determine which models are helpful and so these previously unpublished models have a right to be among the others too.

We have also included an additional sales model, as well as a couple of well-known published consultancy models. The sales profession has much to learn from procurement, and vice versa. The inclusion of a separate section just for sales models could well be an inspiration for future editions!

SECTION 1

Key processes

MODEL 1
PROCUREMENT LIFE CYCLE

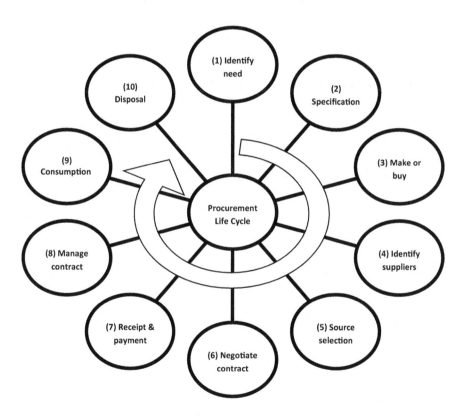

Figure 1.1 Procurement Life Cycle

Overview

This is one of the basic procurement models detailing the main stages of procurement activity when sourcing either goods or services, see Figure 1.1. It begins when

3

a need is identified and ends when that need has been fulfilled and either consumed or disposed of.

The model is cyclical because once a product has been consumed and/or disposed of, a replacement is often required thus repeating the process.

Elements

The main stages of the Procurement Life Cycle are as follows:

Stage 1 – Identify need. The life cycle is initiated with the identification of a need. The business has a requirement and a purchase is required to fulfil it.

Stage 2 – Specification. This is the documented statement of requirements. It is then used by suppliers to assist with technical and pricing decisions.

Stage 3 – Make or buy? The 'make' decision involves the organisation proceeding to fulfil the need internally, whereas the 'buy' decision requires the organisation to purchase from a third party.

Stage 4 – Identify suppliers. This stage involves searching and analysing the supply market; it is about identifying suitable and appropriate resources.

Stage 5 – Source selection. This involves identifying the preferred supplier to supply the goods or services required, possibly through a tendering or RFx exercise.

Stage 6 – Negotiate contract. Once a supplier has been selected there may need to be several rounds of negotiation or clarification in order to agree the final commercial and contractual details.

Stage 7 – Receipt and payment. Payment for goods and services usually occurs after receipt, although this is not always the case. This is often referred to as 'purchasing' or even 'purchase-to-pay' (P2P).

Stage 8 – Manage contract. The contract needs to be managed in order to ensure performance by the supplier. This stage is also sometimes referred to as supply management.

Stage 9 – Consumption. The bought-in goods and serviced are utilised during the life of the contract and may need replenishment, maintenance or some form of service management.

Stage 10 – Decommission and disposal. The end of the life cycle involves the disposal of the product. This is important in view of the drivers for sustainability and whole life costs.

So what?

The Cycle is often used from a theoretical rather than a practical perspective to explain and demonstrate a procurement function's flow of activities. Its form will vary depending on the organisation and its structure.

The model is sometimes referred to as the 'Purchasing Cycle' or the 'Purchase Process' – but these are inadequate descriptions, as the Procurement *Life* Cycle describes the end-to-end stages in the life of both the procurement activity and the purchase itself.

Procurement application

- Identifies the key stages in the procurement process
- Supports business process re-engineering
- Aids the procurement planning process.

Limitations

This is a simple model that shows a process flow. It does not attempt to predict scenarios or indicate potential solutions. There is also some debate as to whether 'procurement' is the correct label for the cycle, with references to purchasing or sourcing instead.

Arguably, the Procurement Life Cycle for public sector organisations may be different from that of private sector organisations because of the requirements of public sector regulated procurement (e.g. WTO rules, EU Directives and so on). However, the Procurement Life Cycle is a generic model that can be adapted to the specific context in which it is to be applied.

Finally, this is seen as having tactical application only, as it does not recognise the more complex and strategic oriented work of the modern procurement function.

Further reading

You can read more about Procurement Life Cycle theory in:

Baily, P., Farmer, D., Crocker, B., Jessop, D. and Jones, D. (2015). *Procurement Principles and Management*. 11th edition. Harlow: Pearson.

Associated models

- Contract Management Cycle (Model 2)
- Category Management Process (Model 3)
- Outsourcing Decision Matrix (Model 26)
- The Negotiation Process (Model 32).

MODEL 2
CONTRACT MANAGEMENT CYCLE

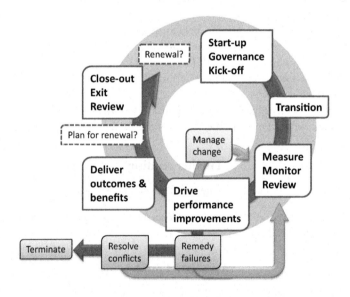

Figure 1.2　Contract Management Cycle

Overview

Managing contracts is one of the hardest and yet most valuable skills required for procurement and commercial practitioners. Too often procurement has been seen as the 'knock it up and run' profession that focuses just on sourcing suppliers and award-ing contracts (and subsequently claiming big paper-based savings) only to leave the management of the contract to others in the organisation. As such, these commercial benefits and savings rarely materialise in full and value often 'walks out of the door' during contract delivery.

The Contract Management Cycle demonstrates the natural lifecycle progression of activities that a contract manager needs to work through when managing a contract and it applies universally across a wide range of contract types.

Elements

There are six main phases in the Contract Management Cycle, plus a number of sub-phases:

Start-up **Governance** **Kick-off**	The initial stages immediately following contract award: • Roles and responsibilities established • Contract Management Plan established • Kick-off meeting held • Pre-commencement requirements fulfilled.
Transition	This represents the mobilisation and ramp-up of activities to full delivery: • Handover completed • Mobilisation of resources • Ramp-up of demand/supply to maturity.
Measure **Monitor** **Review**	Throughout the maturity of the contract, the emphasis is upon performance delivery: • Measuring key performance criteria • Monitoring performance data • Reviewing and interpreting performance • Mitigating risks.
Drive performance improvements	Delivering the required contract performance throughout the life of the contract: • Delivering the required benefits • Compliant with requirements • Continuous improvement gains • Customer satisfaction. Within this the sub-phases of managing change and remedying failures are included.
Deliver outcomes and benefits	Realising the commercial and operational benefits [outcomes] specified within the contract: • Desired outcomes and deliverables • Commercial gains • Social, economic and environmental performance • Ratification of the contract delivery.
Close-out **Exit** **Review**	Preparing for the end of the contract: • Preparing for and managing the exit • Fulfilling termination requirements • Handover to replacement supplier(s) • Learning review for future improvements. This also include the sub-phases of planning for and executing any contract renewals beyond the initial contract term.

Being cyclical, the Contract Management Cycle suggests that these activities recommence with a subsequent (new) contract.

So what?

The Contract Management Cycle encapsulates the full roles and responsibilities of a contract manager (or contract management team) and helps to illustrate these in a simple process diagram. Contract management has clear sequences of activity and several activities naturally flow on from one another. The model helps to map out what the contract manager needs to be focusing on and clearly demonstrates the dynamic nature of contract management.

The next logical progression when using the model is to map roles and responsibilities against key staff and stakeholders, possibly in the form of a RACI matrix so that the organisation can work effectively to ensure that the promised contract deliverables are received effectively.

Procurement application

- Defines key activities for contract managers
- Helps to manage contract deliverables and performance
- Mitigates contractual and commercial risk.

Limitations

Although the Contract Management Cycles offers a systematic and sequential guide to the core activities of contract management, it does not tell you how to manage contracts. The Cycle is a useful listing of activities and helpful for stakeholders to discuss and agree on who does what, however it does not provide any guidance on how better performance from contracts can be delivered.

Contract management is a broad set of commercial skills brought together in this model. However, to deliver tangible and effective results from contract management, you will need to delve deeper into this subject and explore each of these commercial activities individually.

Further reading

The International Association for Contract & Commercial Management (IACCM) is probably the world's leading professional body for contract management and offers a series of professional qualifications and training to support contract managers. You can read more about the cycle of contract management activities in:

Cummins, T. et al. (2011). *Contract & Commercial Management: The Operational Guide*. Zaltbommel, The Netherlands: Van Haren Publishing.
Emery, B. (2013). *Fundamentals of Contract & Commercial Management*. Zaltbommel, The Netherlands: Van Haren Publishing.

Associated models

- Procurement Life Cycle (Model 1)
- Plan–Do–Check–Act Cycle (Model 5)
- Risk Assessment (Model 9)
- Relationship Continuum (Model 21)
- Contract Management Grid (Model 31).

MODEL 3
CATEGORY MANAGEMENT PROCESS

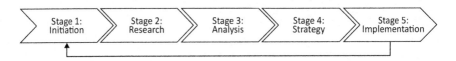

Figure 1.3 Category Management Process

Overview

Category management was first developed in the fast-moving consumer goods (FMCG) sector to help product managers and marketers to group their products together and gain synergies, such as cross-selling and brand leverage. In the 1980s the concept transitioned over to procurement (mainly thanks to Dr Peter Kraljic, see Model 22) where it was recognised that categorising organisational spend made for better management, cost savings and quality improvements.

Category management is defined as 'a continuous process of gathering, analysing and reviewing market data in order to create and execute spend strategies that deliver long-term business benefits' (Cordell and Thompson, 2018). The Category Management Process is therefore an iterative step-by-step process that creates and implements a long-term-plan [strategy] for various groupings of organisational spend, see Figure 1.3.

Elements

There are seven key elements associated with the Category Management Process:

Stage 1 – Initiation. This involves the set up and governance required to scope and bring together cross-functional stakeholders who wish to be involved in shaping and managing the category strategy.

10

Stage 2 – Research. The second stage is about fact-finding and data gathering both internally about the organisational spend and externally about the market. It can be time-consuming, but is worth the research effort.

Stage 3 – Analysis. Once the research has been gathered, it needs to be analysed. This involves a wide range of tools and techniques to understand the nature of the organisational spend, the market and the supply chain. Many of the tools presented elsewhere in this book are used during this stage.

Stage 4 – Strategy. This involves bringing together the research and analysis and applying creative/commercial thought to generate solutions that will manage the organisational spend better. The final strategy often contains several solutions compounded together.

Stage 5 – Implementation. The final stage involves implementing the strategy, managing the associated change and realising the business benefits.

Gateways – Approval check-points are often placed between the stages of the process to ensure that the process runs to plan and that the business is achieving what is needed. These are usually 'go/no-go' check-points.

Continuous improvement – Category management is iterative. Once the first strategy has been developed and implemented, a second generation strategy is required. Improvements are expected to be continuous.

So what?

Category management is a tried and tested management process for building 'breakthrough' strategies. It focuses on the business requirements of the organisational spend and consequently becomes a business-focused methodology, rather than a procurement-focused methodology.

Business benefits can range from quality improvements and service enhancements, through to cost savings, risk mitigation and revenue gain. Category management is a controlled process for bringing about wide cross-functional stakeholder support and building a strategy that is based on facts and data, rather than conjecture or opinion.

Procurement application

*   Identifies key stages in the strategy development process for managing spend
*   Supports spend management
*   Aids the procurement planning process
*   Establishes stakeholder buy-in for procurement plans
*   Delivers major added-value contributions to the business.

Limitations

Unfortunately category management has been taken over by the procurement consultants in recent years and this has given it a bad name. Once in the hands of these consultants, they turn it into a long drawn-out template-filling process where they can bring in expensive associates and bill huge fees.

Because category management is based on data, many organisations lack the appropriate systems to identify accurate spend data and this can inhibit the success of category management. Some category management initiatives end up getting lost in the data gathering, research and analysis phases due to lack of leadership and stakeholder buy-in. The only winners are often the procurement consultants who move on to their next assignment.

Finally, it needs to be pointed out that category management is completely different from 'strategic sourcing'. Category management is not a procurement process per se; its remit is to deliver a strategy, not a sourcing exercise. Category management processes that contain procurement activities by default (like the current CIPS process at the time of writing) are ineffective and badly thought out. There are many more category strategies than just sourcing

Further reading

You can read more about the Category Management Process in:

Cordell, A. and Thompson, I. (2018). *The Category Management Handbook*. Oxford, UK: Routledge.

Associated models

- Procurement Life Cycle (Model 1)
- Strategy Development (Model 12)
- Product Life Cycle (Model 6)
- Kraljic Matrix (Model 22)
- Supplier Categorisation (Model 30).

MODEL 4

COMMUNICATION
PROCESS

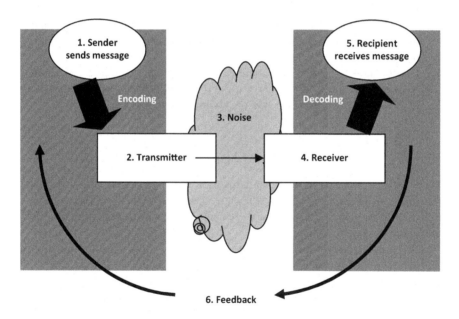

Figure 1.4 Communication Process

Overview

Claude Shannon's (1948) Communication Process is credited with being the forerunner in the modern field of communication models. The model shown in Figure 1.4 introduced the concept of a feedback loop and this version is the one which most others replicate today.

The model illustrates the general process of communication and identifies the key components and their impact upon the message being transmitted.

Elements

Communication requires at least two people – a sender and a recipient. The process through which they do this is as follows:

1. **Sender** – In order to communicate, the sender selects the words to use and the medium for sending, depending on the purpose of the message. This is referred to as 'encoding'.
2. **Transmitter** – The message is sent depending on how it has been prepared and encoded.
3. **Noise** – The environment can interrupt, distort and/or distract from the effectiveness of the communication. This is referred to as 'noise'. Noise reduces the effectiveness of the communication message.
4. **Receiver** – The message is received by the recipient and needs to be interpreted to be understood. This is referred to as 'decoding'.
5. **Recipient** – The recipient is only able to interpret the message as received – after it has been encoded, transmitted through noise and then decoded. As a consequence the received communication may not match the originally intended message.
6. **Feedback** – Ultimately the communication process is completed when the recipient indicates to the sender that the message has been received. This helps the sender to understand whether the communication has been effective.

So what?

Theory suggests that by making communication more effective in the work place, efficiency and productivity levels will remain consistently high. Therefore, an awareness of the process means that potential problems can be spotted at an early stage and can be improved upon as appropriate.

Clear communication processes are essential across a spectrum of organisational activities ranging from public relations to team development.

Given that procurement is a transactional function built on effective relationships and processes, the need for excellent communication should be obvious. The application of excellent communication extends through stakeholder relationships, supplier relationships, negotiation and cross-functional working.

Procurement application

*   Supports procurement marketing in terms of identifying messages to be transmitted and most effective medium
*   Aids communication of functional vision, goals and objectives
*   Facilitates the stakeholder management communications
*   Supports effective negotiation
*   Essential underpinning of category management.

Limitations

The original model was based on telegraph technology and, although the underlying principles still hold, the reality of most modern communication systems is far more complex.

For example, the model assumes a purely dyadic exchange, when most communication in modern organisations needs to involve groups and informal networks.

Advances in technology (such as artificial intelligence) together with more sophisticated business processes (such as game theory) could suggest this model is weak or no longer relevant. As authors we would contend this suggestion. To be effective, electronic communication requires the exact same process and ideally a perfect replica.

Further reading

You can read more about Communication Process theory in:

Boddy, D. (2016). *Management: An Introduction.* 7th edition. Harlow: Pearson.

Associated models

There are several theoretical models associated with the Communication Process, including:

- Category Management Process (Model 3)
- Stakeholder Management Matrix (Model 28)
- The Negotiation Process (Model 32)
- Rapport Matrix (Model 33).

MODEL 5
PLAN–DO–CHECK–ACT

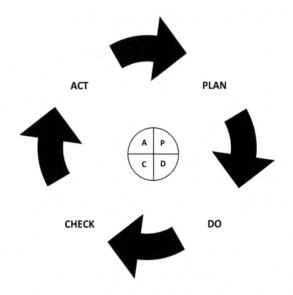

Figure 1.5   PDCA Cycle

Overview

The PDCA Cycle shown in Figure 1.5 was originally developed by scientist Walter A. Shewhart and is sometimes referred to as 'the Shewhart Cycle'. However, it was popularised by W. Edwards Deming (1982) in the 1950s and is consequently known by many as 'the Deming Wheel'. He theorised that this iterative model could assist with the identification and implementation of improvements in relation to production processes.

Elements

The model highlights four key stages (Plan–Do–Check–Act, PDCA) that need to be taken in systematic order:

PLAN – For changes to bring about improvement. Activities could include customer/supplier mapping, flowcharting, Pareto analysis, brainstorming, tender evaluation, supply chain mapping and cause and effect diagrams.

DO – Represents changes that occur. These could be on a small scale first to trial them, or on a wider scale. These could include leadership skills, experimental design, conflict resolution and on-the-job training.

CHECK – To see if the changes are working and to investigate selected processes. Information could include data check-sheets, graphical analysis, control charts, key performance indicators and/or statistical process control.

ACT – To get the greatest benefit from the changes, actions need to be put in place that were observed during the check stage. Actions could include process mapping, process standardisation, controlled reference information and formal training for standard processes, and so on.

The PDCA Cycle is iterative and so after the Act stage, planning should occur for the following iteration of continuous improvement. Thus the model has been linked to the principle of total quality management and also helps to underpin the concepts of lean.

So what?

The PDCA Cycle can be used in a variety of situations:

- Continuous improvement programmes
- Defining and implementing strategy
- Problem solving
- Project management
- New product development
- Business process reengineering
- Lean production/lean supply.

It is often regarded as a simple four-step model for carrying out change and effecting continuous improvement.

Procurement application

- Supports supplier development programmes
- Provides structure for procurement and supply chain projects
- Assists with personal development planning
- Helps build a functional strategy
- Underpins category strategy development.

Limitations

Some academics argue that the model is overly simplistic and outdated. They suggest that the organisations of the 1950s do not adequately reflect the needs of today's global organisations operating in a highly complex and technologically advanced environment. However, the principles of PDCA and continuous improvement are just as relevant today as at any time in our history.

Further reading

You can read more about the PDCA Cycle and Deming's theories in:

Deming, W.E. (1982). *Out of the Crisis*. Cambridge, MA: Massachusetts Institute of Technology, Center for Advanced Educational Services.
Slack, N., Brandon-Jones, A. and Johnston, R. (2016). *Operations Management*. 8th edition. Harlow: Pearson.

Associated models

There are several theoretical models related to the PDCA Cycle, including:

- Category Management Process (Model 3)
- Ishikawa's Fishbone Diagram (Model 8)
- Strategy Development (Model 12)
- Lean Supply (Model 52).

MODEL 6
PRODUCT LIFE CYCLE

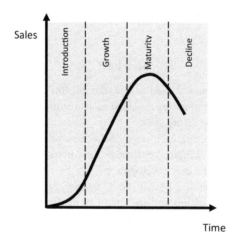

Figure 1.6 Product Life Cycle

Overview

The term 'Product Life Cycle' was first suggested by Theodore Levitt (1965). Theory suggests that when a new product is launched on a market it goes through several growth stages, predicated upon the belief that all products have a limited life-span, which can vary from years to decades as shown in Figure 1.6.

Elements

The Product Life Cycle is divided into four stages, which are defined by revenue generation [sales] and life-span. It can be applied at an individual product or commodity grouping level. These stages are as follows:

Introduction phase – Characterised by heavy investment, this is the stage at which products are launched on to the marketplace and the norm is for slow sales growth accompanied by losses.

Growth phase – Consumers have become aware of and started buying the product; therefore, this stage is characterised by significant increase in demand and profits. However, this will also mean that new competitors could be attracted into the same industry.

Maturity phase – This stage is characterised by decreasing demand as a result of a sales plateau. Often caused by competitors taking larger shares of the market, alternative survival strategies need to be established. The sales plateau could be short-lived (for example with fast-moving technology) or enduring (such as the classic example of *Coca Cola*).

Decline phase – Characterised by a significant reduction in demand and therefore sales and profits, such that a decision needs to be made as to whether to continue with the product. The focus is upon ensuring lowest cost production whilst there is still volume.

So what?

This model has been primarily used as a marketing tool. An awareness of the stage that a product is at can help an organisation to determine its next course of action, such as brand extension or termination.

The approach taken during each stage of the life cycle depends on the nature of the product strategy, for example rapid versus slow market penetration, or the need for market testing before further development.

There is a natural extension of this model to category management, where category managers need to understand the maturity of the products and markets that they are working with and so form a suitable category strategy.

Procurement application

- Planning future sourcing requirements, particularly for new markets/products or for those in decline
- Understanding of suppliers' product/market strategies with a view to joint development and/or continuous improvement programmes
- Enhances business knowledge and thus builds credibility amongst key stakeholders
- Building lasting category strategies.

It should be noted that the Product Life Cycle can also be applied to other contexts, such as the performance curve from a supplier relationship.

Limitations

A major drawback with the Product Life Cycle theory is that it is not predictive. Firms may be able to identify some of the stages of development from historical sales data, but they cannot know their exact position on the cycle, or in which direction they might be heading.

Critics have also argued that the life cycle could become self-fulfilling. For example, if sales peak and then decline, the conclusion may be to assume wrongly that a product is in complete decline altogether, therefore pre-empting any future upsurge in sales (e.g. for seasonal products) by abandoning the product.

Finally, it is important to note that cycle longevity varies greatly. Some products seem to enjoy very long maturity, if not immortality with no signs of decline, whereas others such as 'fad' products could last a matter of months. Some modern technological products challenge the shape of the curve. For example, recent trends in sales of Apple products suggest that there is little or no introduction phase. For these types of product, the life-span is significantly shorter and obsolescence can be a major feature of mature products.

Further reading

You can read more about Product Life Cycle theory in:

Boddy, D. (2016). *Management: An Introduction*. 7th edition. Harlow: Pearson.
Johnson, G., Whittington, R., Scholes, K., Angwin, D. and Regner, P. (2017). *Exploring Strategy: Text and Cases*. 11th edition. Harlow: Pearson.

Associated models

- Ansoff Matrix (Model 14)
- Competition Analysis (Model 15)
- Boston Box (Model 16).

MODEL 7

NETWORK ANALYSIS

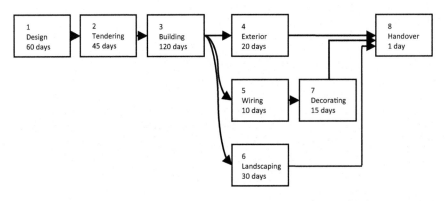

Figure 1.7 Network Analysis Diagram

Overview

Network Analysis is a technique used for planning large or complex projects by rigorously programming and monitoring progress. It is based on the principles of sequencing tasks in a logical order, thus taking a systematic approach to the planning and scheduling of tasks and resources. Figure 1.7 shows a simplified network for the construction of a house.

Network Analysis is regularly used for the development of infrastructure projects, as well as technology development projects (such as software development and/or systems integration) and the execution of implementation plans. It can also be used for procurement projects, such as sourcing activities or the implementation of ordering systems (although these processes are predominantly sequential).

Elements

There are two main forms of Network Analysis: CPA (critical path analysis) and PERT (project evaluation and review technique). Both contain the following elements:

The network – The network is usually an 'activity-on-arrow' diagram (as shown), representing each individual activity within a project with an arrowed line. Events are characterised by their duration and preceding tasks ['predecessors'].

The critical path – The project duration is the time taken to complete the longest path through the network. This is the 'critical path' and activities on it are 'critical activities'. The critical path is the 'bottleneck' route.

Float – Activities that do not lie on the critical path can, within limits, start late or take longer than specified. Slack time associated with a non-critical activity is referred to as 'float' (or sometimes 'buffer'). Some planners build in additional float even on the critical path, but this simply has the effect of increasing the overall project duration.

So what?

Network Analysis is usually associated with the planning and control of large projects in fields such as construction, IT and outsourcing. In addition to the identification of the critical path and therefore timely management of tasks and resources, the model may also be used when comparing incremental costs and benefits.

Network Analysis can be extended to include the necessary resources required for each activity so that the resources can be scheduled, monitored and managed effectively. PERT analysis can also help to determine task duration through estimation and statistical calculation, once the network has been established.

Procurement application

- Supports procurement projects in terms of identifying and managing resources
- Helps ensure contracts are awarded on time
- Aids communication and monitoring of critical activities and deadlines
- Facilitates a smooth operational flow through the supply chain.

Limitations

There has been much debate as to which form of Network Analysis is the superior. It is often posited that PERT is most useful where accurate assessments of likely times are available, but it does not tackle the problems of 'buffered estimates', whereas CPA focuses more on the specific jobs that are critical to the overall project duration.

Any practitioner who has attempted to construct a Network Analysis for a complex set of activities will testify that this can be a time-consuming and complex procedure. Though there are now several off-the-shelf software packages that facilitate this, they can also run the risk of 'hiding' some of the key facts surrounding interdependencies, time estimates and float.

Further reading

You can read more about network analysis in:

Maylor, H. (2010). *Project Management*. 4th edition. Harlow: FT Prentice Hall.
Goldratt, E.M. (1997). *Critical Chain*. Great Barrington, MA: North River Press Publishing Corporation.

Associated models

- The Iron Triangle (Model 45).

MODEL 8
ISHIKAWA'S FISHBONE DIAGRAM

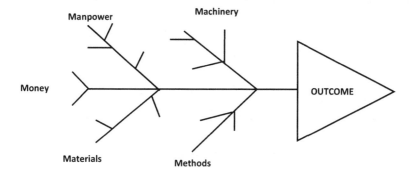

Figure 1.8 Fishbone Diagram

Overview

The Fishbone Diagram, also known as a 'Cause and Effect' diagram shown in Figure 1.8, was developed by Dr Kaoru Ishikawa (1968). It is a simple problem-solving tool often used by quality assurance and continuous improvement teams. The model is used to explore, identify and display the potential root causes of a specific effect – usually a quality outcome or a specific defect of some kind.

Elements

To identify the root cause of a problem, a four-step process is normally applied:

Step 1 – State the problem in the 'outcome box'. For example: 138 ppm defects for a product or 0.7% customer complaints for a service.
Step 2 – Identify the main categories for possible causes of the problem. These form the main branches or 'bones' of the diagram and can be listed under

appropriate headings; although a popular approach is to use the 5 Ms of Manpower, Machinery, Methods, Materials and Money.

Step 3 – Brainstorm the potential causes under each of the headings using facts and data as a basis, together with group discussion.

Step 4 – Record all of the potential causes and narrow them down to the most likely. These are then highlighted in order to indicate items that should be acted upon.

The diagram works from right to left to indicate how the investigation of the causes is 'worked back' from the main outcome back to the root cause itself.

So what?

Ishikawa's Fishbone Diagram is used to explore, identify and display possible cause and effect in any given situation. By pinpointing root problems, it provides quality improvement from the 'bottom up'.

Procurement application

- Supports procurement projects
- Aids continuous improvement teams
- Facilitates quality dialogue with suppliers
- Identifies potential risks in the supply chain.

Limitations

The Fishbone Diagram provides an analytical approach to problem solving that is easy to undertake. However, care must be taken to ensure that the right causes are identified in order to get to the root of the problem, rather than attempting to simultaneously provide solutions that still do not strike at the heart of the problem that needs solving.

Further reading

You can read more about Ishikawa's Fishbone Diagram in:

Ishikawa, K. (2012). *Introduction to Quality Control*. New York: Springer.
Slack, N., Brandon-Jones, A. and Johnston, R. (2016). *Operations Management*. 8th edition. Harlow: Pearson.

Associated models

- Plan–Do–Check–Act (Model 5).

MODEL 9
RISK ASSESSMENT

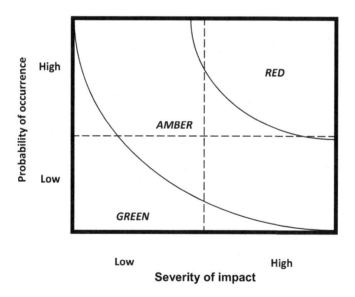

Figure 1.9   Risk Impact Grid

Overview

The Risk Impact Grid shown in Figure 1.9 is a useful means of assessing the magnitude of a risk by looking at the combined effect of its potential impact and the likelihood of it occurring.

Once this assessment has been undertaken, the risks can be nominated to a 'traffic light' red, amber or green coding so that they are easier to monitor and manage.

Priority is given to the 'red' risks to ensure that the risks are managed, whereas 'amber' risks may be monitored closely and 'green' risks only managed by exception.

The coding is relatively arbitrary [within reason] and will depend on the particular user's appetite to risk.

Elements

The key elements of the model are as follows:

Probability of occurrence – Refers to the 'likelihood' of the risk event actually occurring or not. The more likely the event, the higher the magnitude of risk.

Severity of impact – Refers to the impact of the risk event if it actually occurred (in terms of cost, delay or damage). The higher the impact, the higher the magnitude of risk.

Red – Refers to 'high' risks – those that are likely and of high impact. These should be given priority in terms of resourcing and scheduling to manage and, where possible, to mitigate.

Amber – Refers to 'medium' risks – those that are either high impact but not highly probably (or vice versa). These should be monitored very closely and managed/mitigated if resources permit.

Green – Refers to 'low' risks – those that are relatively unlikely and of relatively low impact. These are risks to monitor but not necessarily in need of specific management action to contain or mitigate.

So what?

This is a useful 'pragmatic' model and helps provide a 'rule of thumb' for risk assessment. It helps practitioners think through the assessment and prioritisation of risks so that they can be suitably managed and, eventually, mitigated.

In risk management terms, the model helps to provide an initial risk assessment.

Procurement application

- Provides an initial screening and assessment of risks to a procurement project
- Can be applied to a wide number of procurement activities, including sourcing and supply management
- Provides a consistent and easy-to-understand practice to the management of procurement risks.

Limitations

All the model does is position the risks relative to each other in a graphical format. The model does not identify risks, nor does it conduct the specific assessment of the risk or inform the user how the risk should be managed as a consequence.

However, it is a useful tool and one that is easy-to-adapt into most organisational contexts.

Further reading

You can read more about the Risk Impact Grid in:

Sadgrove, K. (2007). *The Complete Guide to Business Risk Management*. 2nd edition. Aldershot, UK: Gower.

Associated models

There are many complex theoretical models related to the Risk Impact Grid that involve sophisticated methods of risk identification, quantification and management. It should be noted that this model is a practical tool, rather than an academic model and thus there are few equivalent models available for application into the procurement field.

Nevertheless, this is a useful tool and worthy of its place among the top procurement models in use today.

MODEL 10
CARTER'S 10CS OF SUPPLIER APPRAISAL

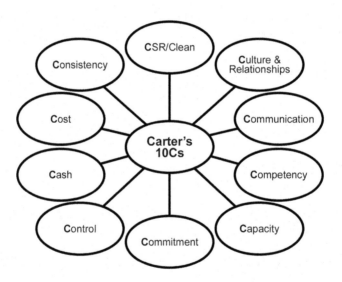

Figure 1.10   Carter's 10Cs

Overview

Dr Ray Carter (1995) first developed his model as a means for appraising potential suppliers during a sourcing process. The original framework only had 7Cs, but the remaining three were subsequently added over time through peer/colleague intervention to form the total shown in Figure 1.10.

The model has become recognised as a useful checklist when undertaking supplier appraisal during the sourcing process, however it can also be used for supplier assessment during the execution of a contract.

Elements

The following 10Cs make up the supplier appraisal checklist:

Competency – Does the supplier have the necessary skills to deliver the goods/services you require?

Capacity – Has the supplier sufficient capacity/flexibility to produce the goods/services? Capacity in this context can include equipment, human resources and materials.

Commitment – Is the supplier committed to maintaining suitable standards and/or suitable procedures and systems?

Control – How does the supplier control its policies, procedures and supply chain?

Cash – Is the supplier in good financial health? What is its financial standing, does it have a positive cash flow or is it over-extended?

Cost – How are the costs of the goods/services made up (i.e. total cost of ownership) and how do these compare with others?

Consistency – How does the supplier guarantee consistency of output in relation to its goods/services?

Corporate Social Responsibility (CSR)/Clean – How committed is the supplier to sustainability, i.e. is the supplier compliant with relevant sustainability legislation?

Culture and relationships – Does the supplier share similar cultural values, i.e. is it a good match/fit?

Communication – How does the supplier communicate with its customers and what communication infrastructure/ICT does it have in place?

So what?

The popularity of this framework comes from its simplicity. It is easily remembered and its application as a checklist is straightforward. The model has often been compared with the much-quoted '5 Rights of Purchasing', and it has been viewed as a more detailed checklist when appraising suppliers prior to entering into potentially long-term relationships.

Procurement application

- Provides a useful checklist of areas to consider when appraising a potential supplier
- Works well with supplier risk assessment
- May be used to assess one's own organisational competence
- Can be applied to suppliers either pre- or post-contract award.

Limitations

Strictly speaking, the model is just a list of things to remember when appraising a supplier during the sourcing process – and not a model. There is no analytical application to it.

It should be noted that the list only really applies to sourcing in the private sector and is not compliant with the current regulations for public sector or utilities contracts due to its confusion of selection and award criteria. A far more sophisticated and useful model for tender evaluation (and one that is compliant with public sector procurement regulation) is the Q:P Tender Evaluation Matrix (Model 11).

The model's evolution is difficult to comprehend and is equally referred to as the 7Cs, 9Cs or 10Cs, depending upon which text book/edition is being referenced. To complicate matters further there are the 9Cs of operational management by an American academic, also named Carter.

Confusion can also arise as a result of the differences in terminology between supplier appraisal and supplier assessment, with the former generally referring to appraisal pre-contract and the latter tending to refer to post-award assessment activity.

Further reading

You can read more about the 10Cs and Carter's other work in:

Carter, R. and Kirby, S. (2006). *Practical Procurement*. Cambridge: Cambridge Academic.

Associated models

- Risk Assessment (Model 9)
- Q:P Tender Evaluation Matrix (Model 11).

MODEL 11
Q:P TENDER EVALUATION

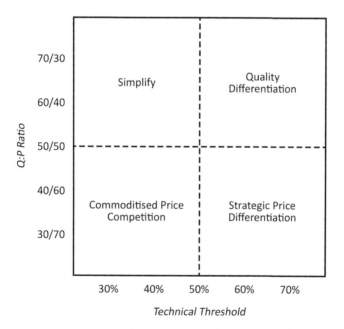

Figure 1.11   The Q:P Tender Evaluation Matrix

Overview

We first came across this incredibly powerful model whilst working with one of the UK's biggest transport utilities. It has been adapted from the Kraljic Matrix (Model 22) to create a design tool for tender evaluation criteria in the public sector. Effectively, the model allows you to simulate the mix of contract award criteria and pick weightings that strategically fit with the type of procurement you are undertaking.

The model helps to determine the best weighting between qualitative factors and price, and also to determine whether a 'minimum' technical threshold is required (and if so at what level).

Elements

The axes represent three related aspects of the award criteria. The vertical axis indicates a sliding scale of the quality/price (Q:P) ratio, with more commoditised [price sensitive] contracts favouring a higher price percentage. The horizontal axis indicates the potential 'minimum' technical threshold required to be considered (i.e. the lowest acceptable quality score).

Thus, there are three broad types of contract to consider:

Commoditised price competition	• Typically these are commoditised goods or services with standard specifications and competitive markets that have little or no differentiation between them • The Q:P ratio favours price over quality • There is no need for a technical threshold as the specification is industry standard • Use these criteria to generate the lowest priced contract • Example: commoditised goods such as stationery, office supplies, etc.
Strategic price differentiation	• Quality is of great importance and a technical threshold is used to indicate the minimum acceptable standard • The technical threshold is relatively high to reflect the high standards of quality required • Once the quality standard is reached, the competition is for the most competitive price • Example: engineered solutions such as IT, construction, etc.
Quality differentiation	• Quality is absolute and the tender is written to encourage the highest possible quality (or greatest innovation) • A high technical threshold is required combined with a Q:P ratio that favours quality over price • Price is secondary to the quality of the service, works or goods required • Use these criteria to drive a higher quality solution • Example: high-end services such as research contracts, creative marketing, advertising, etc.

There is a fourth quadrant on the Q:P Tender Evaluation Matrix suggesting high Q:P ratios with low [negligible] technical thresholds, but this is counter-intuitive and will lead back to one-dimensional competitive tension between quality and price. Accordingly, this quadrant is not used in this model and the suggestion in Figure 1.11 is that purchasers consider simplifying their requirements or simplifying their evaluation approach.

So what?

Public sector purchasers are often left with a conundrum as to the most appropriate balance of award criteria for any given contract. Classic 60:40 or 70:30 Q:P ratios can become default without the purchaser thinking of alternative [more creative] ways of evaluating tenders to get what they want for a contract.

This model particularly helps those in public procurement to design their tender evaluation proactively and therefore shape the competitive solutions they are offered from the market. It also helps give rationalisation to the tender design process when working with non-procurement stakeholders.

Using this model will help to determine the most appropriate evaluation criteria that strategically 'fit' with the goals of the purchase. Effectively purchasers should get better solutions and greater 'value for money' as a result.

Procurement application

- Designs 'fit for purpose' tender evaluation criteria
- Justifies your suggested weightings to stakeholders
- Aligns the tender evaluation with the strategic goals of the business
- Improves tender offerings and value for money.

Limitations

Although the model is a significant step forward for anyone involved in public procurement or tender design, there are practical challenges with each of the criteria within the model.

Price is often perceived as 'absolute' but there are different methods for evaluating and comparing tender prices; this will skew the results.

Similarly, 'quality' is an evaluative score that always has the risk of subjectivity. To be meaningful and effective, the quality scores need to differentiate clearly between 'satisfactory', 'good', 'very good' and 'excellent' grades. A lack of differentiation ends up with ineffective scores for quality and significantly increases the influence of the pricing score.

The technical threshold only becomes effective when there is a range of quality within the market and the purchaser has been able to predict the market's response to the tender requests accurately. There is a risk that the threshold is set too high (thus yielding few or no tenders) or too low (thus bringing in unacceptable quality). The challenge is being able to predict the competitive responses to a tender in advance, which is incredibly difficult in practice.

This leaves the model vulnerable to losing its effectiveness due to poor application in the field, which is a shame because it has a great use if applied correctly.

Associated models

- Carter's 10Cs of Supplier Appraisal (Model 10)
- Kraljic Matrix (Model 22).

SECTION 2

Strategic analysis

MODEL 12
STRATEGY DEVELOPMENT (PCA MODEL)

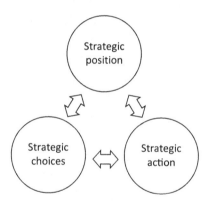

Figure 2.1   PCA Model

Source: adapted from Johnson et al. (2005).

Overview

The PCA Model (Figure 2.1) provides a 'roadmap' for strategy development. Developed by the successful authors on corporate strategy, Gerry Johnson, Kevan Scholes and Richard Whittington (2005), the model originates from their former 'ACI' (analysis, choices, implementation) model of strategy development.

The authors assert that this model should be viewed as a guide to areas for consideration when developing strategy, rather than a prescriptive methodology. The elements are linked in order to highlight their interdependencies, but they do not necessarily pursue a structured step-by-step formula.

Elements

In practical terms, the elements of strategy development do not take a linear form. For example, an understanding of the strategic position may best be built up from previous experience of putting a strategy into action, and so on.

The three key elements can be treated as relatively discrete activities and are made up as follows:

Strategic position – This is concerned with the impact on strategy of the external environment, an organisation's strategic capabilities and the expectations and influence of stakeholders.

Strategic choices – This involves understanding the underlying base for future strategy and the option for developing strategy in terms of direction and methods of development.

Strategic action – This looks at ensuring that strategies are working in practice. Appropriate structuring, support strategies and the management of change are prerequisites for successful implementation.

Each of the above elements is subsequently broken down into three respective sub-components that help to determine the strategy in need of development.

So what?

This model is a relatively simple framework that can be used by anyone wishing to develop and manage a strategy. It is often regarded as the start of the process from which options emerge, but could equally be thought of as a framework to help practitioners develop or refine an existing strategy.

In this regard, it should be remembered that strategy can be developed at a number of levels in an organisation – the functional level (such as procurement), a business unit or divisional level and/or the overall corporate level. The PCA Model is sufficiently flexible to cater for each of these contexts.

There are several theoretical models associated with strategy development, according to which academic's theories you subscribe to. These include:

• Rational planning
• Logical incrementalism
• Emergent strategy

The PCA Model subscribes to the school of logical incrementalism, but there is much validity in considering some of the other approaches too.

Procurement application

• Supports functional strategy planning and development for the procurement function

- Aids team planning sessions
- Generates strategic options for cross-functional projects and teams
- Underpins the category management process.

Limitations

The 'Rational Planning' approach to developing strategy is sometimes preferred because of its logical and formally-documented planning process. This is based on more of a scientific style of management and is driven by facts, data and analysis. However, there is also a realisation that the rational approach does not suit all organisations and it is argued that those that are more dynamic in nature might adopt PCA instead.

One obvious limitation of the PCA approach is that it is not non-prescriptive – in other words, practitioners who want to know what they need to do could be easily frustrated by its lack of instruction and direction.

Further reading

You can read more about the PCA Model in the Johnson et al. (2017) text detailed below. For a useful discussion on wider concepts of strategy development you are encouraged to refer to the Lynch (2018) text detailed below, or any other general strategy text available from good book retailers.

Johnson, G., Whittington, R., Scholes, K., Angwin, D. and Regner, P. (2017). *Exploring Strategy: Text and Cases.* 11th edition. Harlow: Pearson.
Lynch, R. (2018). *Strategic Management.* 8th edition. Harlow: FT Pearson.

Associated models

- Category Management Process (Model 3).

MODEL 13
PORTER'S GENERIC STRATEGIES

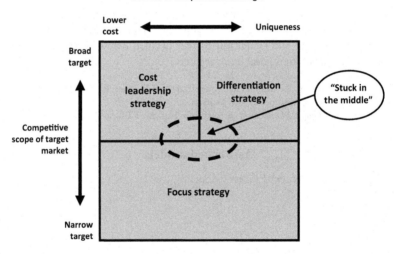

Figure 2.2 Porter's Generic Strategies

Source: adapted from Porter (1980).

Overview

Michael Porter (1980) believed there were three generic competitive strategies that businesses could choose from: cost leadership, differentiation or focus. He suggests that every business needs to select one of these in order to compete in the market place and gain competitive advantage.

This model shown in Figure 2.2 is often used to explore and develop strategy options and can help an organisation to determine its long-term strategic direction.

Elements

An organisation selects its strategy by considering two aspects of the competitive environment:

1. The source of competitive advantage
2. The competitive scope of the target customers.

Porter brought these two aspects together and developed the following three strategies:

Cost leadership – This strategy is based on being the lowest cost producer in the market. It means under-cutting competition and winning market share by offering the lowest prices to customers. The strategy requires support from operations and the supply chain to ensure that the costs of production are kept low at all times.

Differentiation – This strategy is based on providing customers with the perception that the products and services offered are noticeably better. This is achieved by offering additional functionality, better service, superior quality and/or greater technological advancement. The strategy requires support from marketing, operations and the supply chain to maintain the 'superior' differentiation in order to charge a premium.

Focus – This strategy concerns selling into a narrow market and therefore creating a 'niche' for the organisation. Niche strategies can have either a low cost focus or a differentiation focus. Support is required from marketing operations and the supply chain to ensure the requirements of the niche are provided for overall.

So what?

There is a lot of discussion between strategists about the risks or advantages of being 'stuck in the middle' (i.e. where a firm engages in each generic strategy, but fails to achieve any single one of them). Porter saw this as disadvantageous, claiming that the organisation is unable to compete effectively in either segment and therefore will be much less profitable.

However, contemporary practice by many leading brands, such as Toyota for example, has demonstrated that competitive advantage can be successfully sustained by products that are differentiated and yet have low costs too.

Procurement application

- Supports the development of procurement strategy
- Assists supplier and supply market analysis

- Enhances business knowledge and thus helps to build credibility amongst internal stakeholders.

Limitations

The model is purely descriptive in that it provides three strategic options for strategists to choose between, rather than analysing a given situation and/or informing which strategy is best to select.

There have been several criticisms of Porter's approach based on empirical evidence of actual industry practice that suggest the three generic strategies are insufficient. Undoubtedly these comments have some validity, but the generic strategies still represent a useful starting point in developing strategic options.

Further reading

You can read more about Porter's Generic Strategies theory in:

Porter, M.E. (1980). *Competitive Strategy: Techniques for Analysing Industries & Competitors*. New York: The Free Press
Lynch, R. (2018). *Strategic Management*. 8th edition. Harlow: Pearson.

Associated models

- Competition Analysis (Model 15)
- Boston Box (Model 16)
- SWOT Analysis (Model 17).

MODEL 14
ANSOFF MATRIX

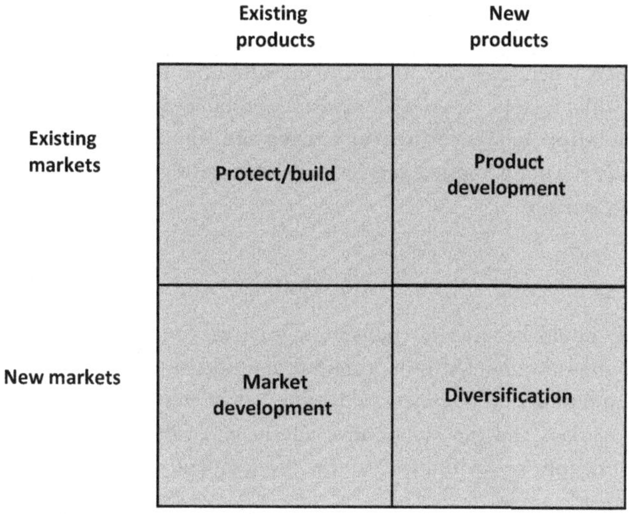

	Existing products	New products
Existing markets	Protect/build	Product development
New markets	Market development	Diversification

Figure 2.3   Strategic Choices

Source: adapted from Ansoff (1957).

Overview

Igor Ansoff's (1957) 'strategic choices' matrix, Figure 2.3, was first published in the *Harvard Business Review* in 1957 and has stood the test of time as one of the most respected strategic models. As a form of portfolio management, it provides strategic product and market growth choices for an organisation. Markets are defined as customers, whereas products are defined as the items that are sold to the customers.

This matrix is a method of generating strategic options for organisations; however, it can also be used to assess competitor's products/markets in order to gain 'first mover advantage'.

Elements

The Ansoff Matrix enables an organisation to choose from a combination of four options to best suit its needs and to provide for optimum growth success. The four options are as follows:

Protect/build – This focuses on protecting and building the company's present position, through either consolidation of current products or through opportunities for market penetration (growing market share in an existing market).

Product development – This focuses on delivering new products to an existing market, either for survival of the organisation or to take advantage of opportunities that have opened up through a changing market.

Market development – This focuses on breaking into new markets with existing products when there are no further opportunities in a current market. Examples would include new uses for existing products or new geographical areas.

Diversification – This focuses on moving the company away from its current product portfolio and markets to increase its revenue by selling new products in new markets.

So what?

This model should be used for generating strategic product and market options. When applying this model, it is important to consider the dynamics in the relationship between product development and a number of factors, including the potential size of the markets and the competitive advantage of the organisation. Synergy is required to identify opportunities for the development of complementary, new or existing market activities.

This model may also be used with different axes such as strategies (existing and new) versus markets (existing and new); or strategies (existing and new) versus products (existing and new). These variations help assess strategic options for the organisation going forward and are based on the same principles as the original Ansoff Matrix.

Procurement application

- Planning future sourcing requirements, particularly for new markets/products or for those in decline
- Understanding of suppliers' product/market strategies with a view to joint development and/or continuous improvement programmes

- Enhancing business knowledge and thus building credibility amongst key stakeholders
- Supporting the development of a category strategy.

Limitations

This matrix does not in itself provide indicators of which option to choose in what circumstances. It is purely for 'options generation' rather than evaluation. Some theorists also argue that the options generated are more likely to be considered by profitable companies rather than those attempting to recover from substantial losses.

Many have challenged the axes of the Ansoff Matrix arguing that the definitions of 'market' and 'product' are too imprecise for modern-day business and therefore the model is outdated.

Finally, critics have also suggested that this model lends itself more to the commercial sector rather than the not-for-profit and/or public sectors.

Further reading

You can read more about the competitive environment and Ansoff's theories in:

Ansoff, H.I. (1984). *Implementing Strategic Management*. Englewood Cliffs, NJ: Prentice-Hall International.

Johnson, G., Whittington, R., Scholes, K., Angwin, D. and Regner, P. (2017). *Exploring Strategy: Text and Cases*. 11th edition. Harlow: Pearson.

Associated models

- Porter's Generic Strategies (Model 13)
- SWOT Analysis (Model 17).

MODEL 15

COMPETITION ANALYSIS

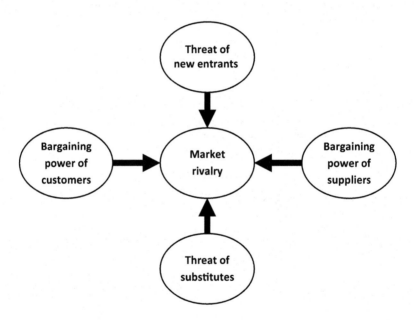

Figure 2.4   Five Forces of Competition
Source: adapted from Porter (1980).

Overview

Michael Porter (1980) originally developed the Five Forces model, Figure 2.4, as a way of evaluating the attractiveness (profit potential) of an industry. He described his analysis as being concerned with the 'forces driving industry competition'.

This model is a useful tool when undertaking industry analysis and can aid the strategy development process. Assessing all facets of potential competition provides for a rounded view when deciding upon what action to take in order to gain a competitive advantage.

Elements

In any industry, whether it is domestic or international or whether it produces a product or a service, the rules of competition are embodied in five competitive forces that Porter classified as follows:

Threat of new entrants – This relates to the competitive pressures placed by new entrants to a market and the degree to which this can be prevented by *Barriers to Entry* (which are factors that new entrants to the market will need to overcome to be successful).

Bargaining of suppliers – Where demand exceeds supply, the supply-base will have greater bargaining power over buyers – particularly if there are no alternative sources of supply. It is essential to reduce as much dependency and competitive pressure on the organisation as possible.

Bargaining power of customers – Where supply exceeds demand from customers, or the demand is heavily consolidated, additional pressures will be placed upon the market. This will increase competition and reduce prices unless the customers' bargaining power can be negated.

Threat of substitutes – Alternative products and services increase competitive pressures on a market, simply because it reduces the customers' dependency and gives them more opportunity to switch to alternatives.

Market rivalry – Competition within the market will depend on just how saturated and/or dynamic the market is.

So what?

Increased competition drives down the profit potential in a market. Organisations therefore need to understand how to develop opportunities in their environment and protect against competition and other threats.

Correct application of this model is at business unit level rather than across the whole organisation, as it is considered that many large firms compete simultaneously in several different environments.

Procurement application

- Planning and preparing for a negotiation by determining market dynamics
- Assisting with sourcing decisions, such as make or buy
- Analysis of the supplier's market and supply chain forces
- Supporting future sourcing plans and category strategies.

Limitations

This model has been the subject of some critical comment, largely surrounding the static nature of the framework, whereas in practice the competitive environment is constantly changing.

It has also been argued that the model ignores human resource aspects of corporate strategy such as country cultures and management skills.

One of the greatest critics from the procurement field has been Professor Andrew Cox who has published strong criticism of the model (Cox, 2014). His analysis is a welcome contribution to the debate on competitive strategy.

This model is one of the most popular models in business schools today and has made itself into the category management toolkits of almost all larger procurement teams. However, the application of the model is at times weak, with many practitioners and consultants confusing themselves between the market and the suppliers. It should not be too hard to make the distinction: the market refers specifically to the market that is being analysed for competitive forces, whereas the suppliers refer to the supply market that is serving that market. For procurement practitioners analysing their supplier's markets (i.e. tier one of their supply chain), the suppliers of Porter's model therefore refer to second tier suppliers. Any other interpretation just does not make sense.

Further reading

You can read more about the competitive environment and Porter's theories in:

Porter, M.E. (1980). *Competitive Strategy: Techniques for Analysing Industries & Competitors.* New York: The Free Press.
Johnson, G., Whittington, R., Scholes, K., Angwin, D. and Regner, P. (2017). *Exploring Strategy: Text and Cases.* 11th edition. Harlow: Pearson.
Cox, A. (2014). *Sourcing Portfolio Analysis.* Boston, UK: Earlsgate Press.

Associated models

There are several theoretical models associated with competitive forces, including:

- SWOT Analysis (Model 17)
- PESTLE (Model 18)
- Power-Dependency Model (Model 24).

MODEL 16
BOSTON BOX

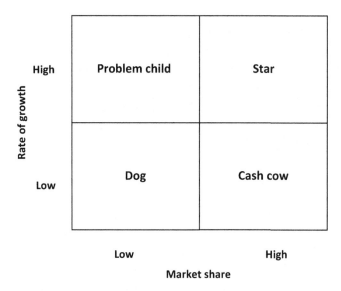

Figure 2.5   BCG Matrix

Source: adapted from Henderson (1984).

Overview

Figure 2.5 was developed in the mid-1980s by the Boston Consulting Group (BCG) and is commonly known as the 'Boston Box'. It is a means of analysing an organisation's product portfolio in terms of relative market share and rate of growth.

By reviewing the relationship between these two factors, an organisation is able to identify the potential success of its product(s) in the market place, and therefore plan accordingly to invest (or divest).

Elements

The horizontal axis of the matrix is represented by market share. This serves as a measure of the strength of a product within the market; while the vertical axis of the matrix represents market growth rate share, which provides a measure of market attractiveness.

The four types of product rating are as follows:

Star – High share products operating in high growth markets. Because they are in a high growth market, they will require a large investment, although the fact that they have a large market share means that economies of scale could be sought.

Cash cow – High market share, but in low growth markets. These are usually established products requiring little investment to perform well and make a profit. This profit can then be transferred to 'Star' products.

Problem child – Products with low market share in high growth markets. This may mean that the product actually starts costing the company money, and therefore work needs to be undertaken to maximise its potential.

Dog – Low market share in low growth markets. Products placed in this section are declining and should not be invested in, as they will not make a profit.

So what?

This model allows organisations to focus on planning the future for their portfolio of products and enables them to define their priorities and strategies depending on the results.

The generally agreed actions arising from the use of the model are to invest profit obtained from the cash cows into the 'stars' and new products as well as some 'problem children' with the aim of turning them into stars.

It also serves to raise questions about products that are labelled as 'dogs' within an organisation and the action required to address these issues.

Procurement application

- Planning future sourcing requirements for potentially high demand products, such as rising stars
- Understanding of suppliers' portfolios and hence identifying potential cost reduction opportunities on products, such as those that could be in decline
- Building dynamic category strategies
- Enhanced business knowledge and thus build credibility amongst stakeholders.

Limitations

There is a number of problems associated with the model. The most obvious is that planning product strategy is defined in terms of only market share and growth rate and other factors are ignored. Also, there is no set definition of market growth or market share, which therefore makes the accuracy of the results questionable.

Further reading

You can read more about the Boston Box in:

Henderson, B.D. (1984). *The Logic of Business Strategy*. New York: Ballinger Publishing Co.
Johnson, G., Whittington, R., Scholes, K., Angwin, D. and Regner, P. (2017). *Exploring Strategy: Text and Cases*. 11th edition. Harlow: Pearson.

Associated models

There are several theoretical models associated with the Boston Box, including:

- Product Life Cycle (Model 6)
- Ansoff Matrix (Model 14).

MODEL 17
SWOT ANALYSIS

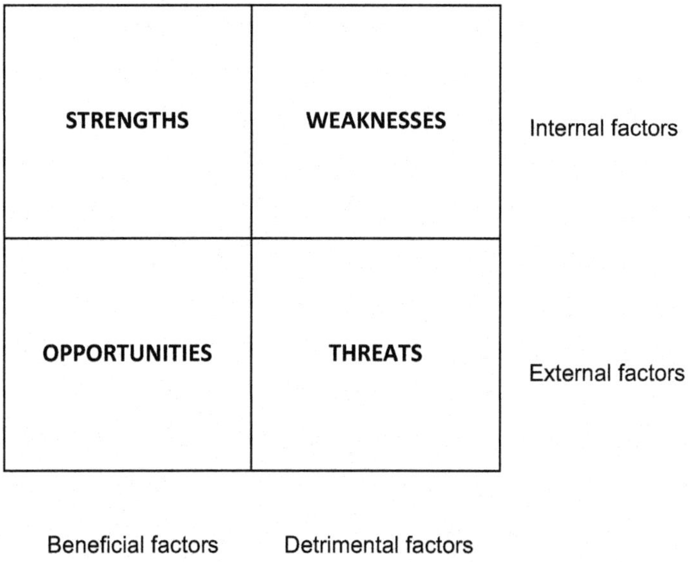

| STRENGTHS | WEAKNESSES | Internal factors |
| OPPORTUNITIES | THREATS | External factors |

Beneficial factors Detrimental factors

Figure 2.6   SWOT Analysis

Overview

SWOT Analysis emanated from the Stanford Research Institute in the mid-1960s. The model shown in Figure 2.6 is a mnemonic (for strengths, weaknesses, opportunities and threats) representing the factors for analysis when assessing a business or a proposition. It is a subjective assessment of data that is organised by the SWOT format into a logical order.

Elements

SWOT Analysis necessitates an understanding both of the organisation's environment and of its resource capabilities. The matrix is divided into four key areas:

Strengths – These are positive internal attributes, for example highly skilled staff, intellectual property rights and/or brand.

Weaknesses – These are the internal weaknesses of the organisation, for example high overheads, old technology and/or poor internal processes.

Opportunities – These are external factors that could influence the organisation, for example a supplier with an opportunity to introduce cost savings.

Threats – These are external risk factors, for example the threat of competition.

So what?

SWOT Analysis is normally used in conjunction with a range of other analytical tools as part of an overall strategic decision-making process.

It is often used to evaluate competitors; however, it can also be used for self-development purposes.

Procurement application

- Helps to highlight an organisation's strengths to help encourage negotiators, but also to highlight possible weaknesses and thus risks that need to be explored in a negotiation
- Helps to determine what opportunities may be available and to follow these as soon as possible
- Helps to highlight potential threats from competitors or the external environment early, so as to avoid or reduce their effect
- By looking at both the suppliers and your own organisation through the SWOT Analysis, you can determine the relative strengths/weaknesses and plan your actions accordingly.

Limitations

SWOT is purely a 'snap shot' in time of the status quo. It does not provide direction or next steps. Some critics have argued that SWOT is not really an analytical tool and that it is purely a framework to structure facts and data concerning the current situation.

It should be noted that there is overlap between SWOT and PESTLE (Model 18), albeit SWOT considers both internal and external factors, whereas PESTLE only considers external influences.

Further reading

You can read more about SWOT Analysis in:

Johnson, G., Whittington, R., Scholes, K., Angwin, D. and Regner, P. (2017). *Exploring Strategy: Text and Cases.* 11th edition. Harlow: Pearson.
Boddy, D. (2016). *Management: An Introduction.* 7th edition. Harlow: Pearson.

Associated models

Other models associated with SWOT Analysis include:

- Ishikawa's Fishbone Diagram (Model 8)
- Strategy Development (Model 12)
- Ansoff Matrix (Model 14)
- Competition Analysis (Model 15)
- PESTLE (Model 18).

MODEL 18
PESTLE

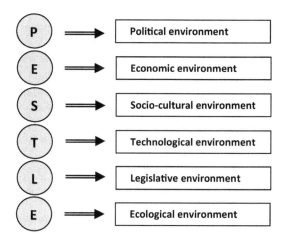

Figure 2.7   PESTLE

Overview

'PESTLE' (which stands for political, economic, socio-cultural, technological, legislative and ecological, as shown in Figure 2.7) is a framework representing the macro-environmental factors that need to be considered when analysing an organisation. It is an analytical model used particularly in relation to strategic planning, market positioning, category management or product development.

Each of the letters within the 'PESTLE' framework represent a different factor within the external environment that, although beyond the organisation's direct control, still is of influence upon its activities.

The framework tends to be over-used within the business schools and has taken on many different forms over the years, including: PEST (political, economic, socio-cultural and technological), SLEPT (socio-cultural, legislative, economic, political and technological) and STEEPLE (socio-cultural, technological, economic, ecological, political, legislative and ethical), amongst others. These differences are relatively minor as each variant seems to incorporate the others' elements in some shape or form. One professional body is even considering STEEPLED (with the addition of demographics) but this only confuses with socio-cultural factors.

Elements

Each of the PESTLE factors varies in significance depending upon the industry sector, however in general terms the elements are as follows:

Political environment – This includes issues such as local and national government actions, trade relations and political stability.

Economic environment – Looks at fiscal policies such as taxes, lending/exchange rates and inflation.

Socio-cultural environment – This highlights the importance of demographics, society and culture on a business.

Technological environment – Focuses on the rate of innovation and diffusion as well as the development of technical standards.

Legislative environment – This covers legislation and regulations, including aspects of governance, contracts, compliance and public accountability.

Ecological environment – This covers the influence of the natural world and awareness of the demand for raw materials and the use of energy, as well as disposal of waste.

So what?

The PESTLE template promotes proactive thinking rather than reliance upon habitual or instinctive reactions. By defining each environmental factor, this allows for a detailed review of potential impacts upon an organisation.

A PESTLE analysis can help to identify SWOT factors (Model 17) and support the analysis required to understand an organisation's strategic position when developing strategies.

Procurement application

- Supports analysis preparation prior to a negotiation
- Aids understanding of supplier organisations
- Builds general commercial awareness
- Helps to develop the category strategy.

Limitations

It is important to identify and define the subject of a PESTLE analysis clearly, otherwise the resulting output could be too wide and varied to assess.

Many academics prefer the original PEST model, as it is thought that it puts more pressure on strategic appreciation and analysis than a longer list of headings. Attempts at the continued widening of the model (such as our reference to STEEPLED earlier) move beyond the realms of credibility and perhaps suggest more about the limited understanding of the protagonists than anything else.

Either way, it should be noted that this model is merely a list of headings as opposed to having any analytical or predictive qualities. It provides a useful guide and *aide memoire*, but should not be relied on for much more than this.

Further reading

You can read more about PESTLE and the macro-environmental factors it highlights in:

Boddy, D. (2016). *Management: An Introduction.* 7th edition. Harlow: Pearson.

Baily, P., Farmer, D., Crocker, B., Jessop, D. and Jones, D. (2015). *Procurement Principles and Management.* 11th edition. Harlow: Pearson.

Cordell, A. and Thompson, I. (2018) *The Category Management Handbook.* Abingdon, UK: Routledge.

Associated models

Other models associated with macro-environmental analysis include:

- Competition Analysis (Model 15)
- SWOT Analysis (Model 17).

MODEL 19
PUSH–PULL INVENTORY STRATEGY

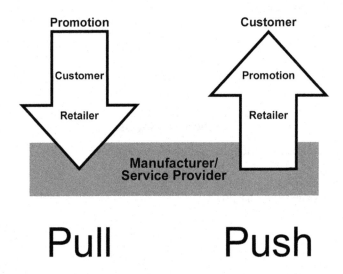

Figure 2.8   Push–Pull

Overview

The Push–Pull Inventory Strategy, Figure 2.8, is based on supply chain 'flow' principles that allow companies to determine whether their business requires a 'push' or 'pull' inventory system.

The pull concept is essentially the *kanban* signal approach, where demand at the customer end of the supply chain pulls product towards the consumer market, supported by a flow of components and resources determined by the same demand.

In contrast, the push concept occurs where products are manufactured in batches for stockpiling, with the view that demand for the product will be created once there is supply.

Elements

There are two main elements:

Pull system – Based on the control of the pace and specification of what is required being set by the customer, which then pulls the work from the operations and it supporting supply chain. The customer is the trigger for the movement between these systems. If there is no request, then the supplier should not produce anything or move any materials.

When a request is put in from a customer [demand] this then triggers production 'on demand', which prompts the supply chain to deliver the requirement.

Push system – Activities and controls are scheduled by a central production system and are in line with centralised instructions. Each work centre pushes out the product in accordance with a pre-planned production schedule, without considering if the succeeding work centre can make use of it or if there is demand for the product at the customers' end. This can cause unnecessary inventory costs, but can also help build capacity for excessive utilisation.

So what?

The pull system is based upon demand being created from the customer. The demand is then transmitted through the stages from the original point of demand by the customer. This creates an efficient 'on demand' production system and supply chain, but assumes that capacity can always match demand.

Conversely, the push system is based upon pushing products into the market irrespective of the demand for the product. This can result in surplus stock and time and money being spent on a product, which may or may not be required.

Procurement application

- Enables more accurate matching of supply and demand
- Helps to determine optimum production scheduling
- Allows for efficient supply chain management
- Can improve supplier relations
- Helps to lower the total cost of production through removal of waste and inefficiency.

Limitations

Push–Pull Inventory strategies are mainly used as an overarching guide to determine the flow in the supply chain and assist with supply chain scheduling. The model helps identify which strategy is most suited to your supply chain and enables you to see which method would be most appropriate. In reality, techniques such as demand forecasting and supply chain optimisation are complex subjects that cannot simply be addressed in these relatively simplistic ways.

Further reading

You can read more about the Push–Pull Inventory Strategy in:

Slack, N., Brandon-Jones, A. and Johnston, R. (2016). *Operations Management*. 8th edition. Harlow: Pearson.
Christopher, M. (2005). *Logistics and Supply Chain Management: Creating Value-Adding Networks*. 3rd edition. Harlow: FT Prentice Hall.

Associated models

- Lean vs. Agile Supply (Model 52).

MODEL 20
SOURCING GEMSTONE

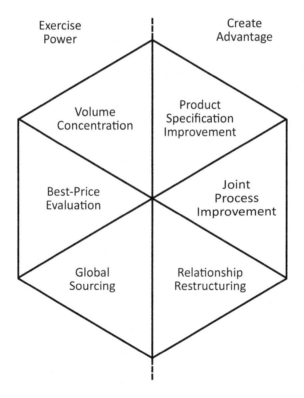

Figure 2.9   Sourcing Gemstone

Source: adapted from Clegg and Montgomery (2005).

Overview

The Sourcing Gemstone was developed in 2001 by the consultancy AT Kearney as a tool to help determine the most appropriate sourcing strategy for any given purchase (or category), see Figure 2.9.

It offers an alternative to the Kraljic Matrix (Model 22) without all of the complexities and inconsistencies of the Purchasing Chessboard (Model 25) and offers six broad strategies for purchasers to consider.

To understand how the model determines the right sourcing strategy, an analysis of the supply market complexity is required. This leads the user to one of three strategies to choose from, depending on whether to exercise power over the supply market or to work collaboratively with the supply market to create mutual advantage.

Elements

The six sourcing strategies derived from the Sourcing Gemstone can be described as follows:

Strategies for exercising power over the supply market:

Volume concentration	• Supplier rationalisation
	• Volume aggregation
	• Redistribution of order volumes
Best-price evaluation	• Price-based sourcing
	• Whole-life costing & 'should cost'
	• Price renegotiation
Global sourcing	• Expand global sources
	• Develop new suppliers
	• Exploit global opportunities

Strategies for creating mutual advantage with the supply market:

Product specification improvement	• Value analysis/value engineering
	• Standardise specifications
	• Content substitution
Joint process improvement	• Business reengineering
	• Integrate operational processes
	• Share productivity gains
Relationship restructuring	• Supplier relationship management
	• Establish strategic alliances
	• Make versus buy

Source: adapted from AT Kearney.

So what?

The Sourcing Gemstone has served its purpose well in the development of 'strategic procurement' with a modern twist on the Kraljic Matrix. It recognises the importance of flexing your sourcing strategy according to the nature of the supply market and it provides practitioners with a useful range of strategies to consider.

The strategies for exercising power are based on the adoption of competitive leverage over the market, where the buyer can exert their economic power to exploit commercial opportunities. Conversely the strategies for creating mutual advantage require collaboration with the supply market, where power is more equally shared.

Procurement application

- Helps to determine which sourcing strategy to adopt
- Provides a range of strategic options to choose from
- Gives insight into methods for extracting value from the supply market.

Limitations

Although the Sourcing Gemstone provides a range of strategic sourcing options, it does not provide an effective methodology for how to make the right choice.

In reality the model is simply a set of two lists: those for competitive leverage scenarios and those for collaboration. The only distinction between these two lists is a rather flimsy adaptation of the Kraljic Matrix based on 'supply market complexity'. It does not take a genius to realise that determining a sourcing strategy requires a lot more than this. This could possibly explain why the Purchasing Chessboard (Model 25) was later developed by the same consulting firm.

The two sets of sourcing strategies have a number of obvious gaps within them and, most importantly, they offer no guidance for dealing with issues of supply dependency (i.e. where a dominant supplier is exerting its power on the buyer).

Further reading

You can read more about the Sourcing Gemstone in:

Clegg, H. and Montgomery, S. (2005). Seven steps for sourcing information products. *Information Outlook*, 9(12), December.

Associated models

- Kraljic Matrix (Model 22)
- Power–Dependency Model (Model 24)
- Purchasing Chessboard (Model 25)
- Outsourcing Decision Matrix (Model 26).

SECTION 3

Relationships

MODEL 21

RELATIONSHIP CONTINUUM

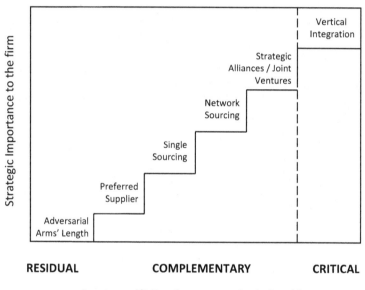

Figure 3.1 Relationship Continuum

Source: adapted from Cox (1996).

Overview

The concept of a continuum of internal and external contractual relationships has been common to applied economics for many decades. It relates to *transaction cost economics* and the theory that the 'boundary of the firm' is driven by the economic costs of transactions, relative to the overall value of the goods/services required.

The growth of the procurement profession during the late twentieth century witnessed a development of these theories and, in particular, the emergence of the 'contingency' approach to contractual relationships. In other words, there is a range of different business relationships from which one type of relationship is going to be optimal for an organisation's needs in any given contingent circumstance – rather than just one best relationship for all situations.

The Relationship Continuum (shown in Figure 3.1) identifies the full range of business relationships, stretching from the most arms' length (and adversarial) through to those that are close-working (and collaborative).

This was adapted from the theory of relational competence (developed by Professor Andrew Cox, 1996), which suggests that the natural extension to the closest working relationship is an internal relationship, thus determining the 'boundary of the firm'.

Elements

There are many different forms of the Relationship Continuum. Cox's Relational Competence Model (1996) is one of the better developed models and comprises the following elements:

Adversarial arms' length refers to 'market based' business relationships that are generally competitive and tactical in nature.

Preferred supplier refers to selected buyer-supplier relationships where there is a degree of shared working and account management.

Single sourcing refers to a relationship where the vendor has been selected to the exclusivity of all others, therefore making them a chosen 'partner' of the buyer's organisation.

Network sourcing refers to co-operative working in supplier networks and alliances, where all parties are interdependent and work together collaboratively.

Strategic alliances/joint ventures refer to interdependent supply relationships of 'co-destiny' – often incorporating shared investment or capital funding.

Vertical integration refers to the internal relationships found between internal service providers and their user/purchaser counterparts.

So what?

It stands to reason that there will be different forms of commercial relationship available to the buyer and that the choice may change for differing circumstances. The Relationship Continuum identifies the full spectrum available and helps the buyer to think through the degree of competitive positioning vis-à-vis collaborative working that needs to be established with the supplier.

Procurement application

- Helps to identify the optimal type of contractual relationship.
- Helps to determine the level of collaboration and/or competition that is required to make the relationship fulfil its required business objectives.

- Helps determine which relationships are most important to the buyer's organisation and therefore which need the most resource and careful management.
- Helps buyers work up a coherent (and dynamic) category strategy.

Limitations

For many practitioners, knowing that there is a range of different buyer–supplier relationships at hand is insufficient – this is common sense. Practitioners need simple and effective tools to help them choose which type of relationship is best.

The theory surrounding Relationship Competence and the Relationship Continuum is complex and, at times, inaccessible to most (because of the unnecessarily complicated manner in which it is presented). Therefore, simplified models of the Relationship Continuum have been developed over time by various practitioners, consultants and professional bodies. The danger with these cut-down models is that they become simplistic and fallacious. Practitioners should decide whether to stick to alternative models, such as that provided by Kraljic (1983, as per Model 22) or to invest time reading up on the academic theories supporting these models.

Further reading

You can read more about Relational Competence and the Relationship Continuum in:

Cox, A. (1996). Relational competence and strategic procurement management: towards an entrepreneurial and contractual theory of the firm. *European Journal of Purchasing & Supply Management*, 2(1), 57–70.
Lysons, K. and Farrington, B. (2012). *Purchasing & Supply Chain Management*. 8th edition. Harlow: FT Prentice Hall.

Associated models

- Sourcing Gemstone (Model 20)
- Kraljic Matrix (Model 22)
- Power-Dependency Model (Model 24)
- Purchasing Chessboard (Model 25)
- Outsourcing Decision Matrix (Model 26).

MODEL 22
KRALJIC MATRIX

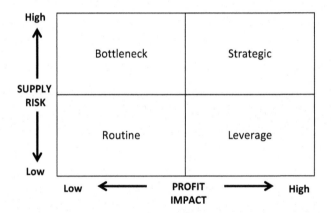

Figure 3.2 Kraljic Matrix

Source: adapted from Kraljic (1983).

Overview

Dr Peter Kraljic (1983) was the first academic to bring portfolio models into the procurement arena. He developed his matrix shown in Figure 3.2 in the early 1980s, with the aim of demonstrating how much time (and resource) buyers should focus on managing different categories of expenditure within an organisation.

The matrix is based on two dimensions; a simplified classification of an organisation's expenditure on goods and services in terms of the profit impact and supply risk.

Over time this model has earned a prime place in the procurement 'hall of fame' as one of the seminal pieces of theory that all junior buyers should know.

Elements

The two key dimensions can be defined as follows:

- **Profit impact** – the strategic importance of purchasing in terms of the value added by the product line, the percentage of raw materials in total costs and their impact on profitability.
- **Supply risk** – the complexity of the supply market gauged by supply scarcity, pace of technology and/or materials substitution, entry barriers, logistics cost or complexity, and monopoly or oligopoly conditions.

These dimensions are used to determine how the expenditure might be managed:

Bottleneck – Products that can only be acquired from a limited source of supply or where there is a high degree of supply risk. Suppliers need to be managed in order to secure delivery. This quadrant is typically characterised by bespoke/rolling contracts and contingency sources of supply to manage the risk.

Strategic – Products that are crucial to the firm and are characterised by high value and high supply risk. Suppliers need to be closely managed. This quadrant is typically characterised by strategic partnering relationships.

Routine – Products that are easy to acquire and also have a relatively low impact in the event of non-delivery. The buyers' efforts should concentrate on implementing standardised ordering procedures and improving efficiency. This quadrant is typically characterised by volume/blanket agreements and/or routine transactional purchasing, such as e-catalogues or purchase cards.

Leverage – Products that are easy to buy and which could result in significant cost savings due to high volume/values, thus greatly impacting contribution to the bottom line. This quadrant is characterised by many suppliers and quality is standardised therefore encouraging frequent competitive tendering and/or leverage-based negotiation.

So what?

Kraljic's Matrix is used extensively within the procurement and supply chain arena. It is often carried out at the planning stages when developing a sourcing strategy for either the function or individual categories of expenditure.

Some debate has been generated about whether the model assesses categories of expenditure or individual supplier relationships. Although Kraljic intended the former, there is some application to the latter in specific [more limited] circumstances.

Many consulting firms have adapted and/or oversimplified Kraljic's Matrix in an attempt to pass off the model as their own. Although it has sometimes been referred to as 'Supply Positioning' and been attributed different titles for its quadrants, this is just a copy and the principles laid down by Kraljic remain the same.

Procurement application

- Assists the development of procurement and category strategies
- Aids both supplier and supply market analysis
- Supports spend analysis
- Provides focus to supplier management activities.

Limitations

Kraljic's Matrix has generated much discussion and debate with some claiming it a panacea and others considering it to be extremely limited in application.

The model is only a 'snapshot' in time and from a practical perspective it does not consider the resources needed to appropriately manage the suppliers of the products in each of the quadrants.

Some academics have argued that the axis definitions need to be precise in order to collate meaningful data and that too much subjectivity can occur when application occurs. Linked to this, one sustained criticism is that this model is only based on the buyer's perspective of the purchases.

Some consulting firms believe the axes should be graded and consequently items can be plotted on the matrix like a statistical graph – but this is probably an extension too far beyond Kraljic's original intentions and there are risks inherent in this approach.

Finally, some believe that the four quadrants can be represented linearly along the Relationship Continuum (as in Model 21) to express the full range of contractual relationships with suppliers – but again there are some grave oversimplifications and fallacies with this type of approach.

Further reading

Kraljic originally published his theory in the article: 'Purchasing must become Supply Management' in *Harvard Business Review* (September–October, 1983). You can read more about Kraljic's purchasing portfolio matrix in:

Lysons, K. and Farrington, B. (2012). *Purchasing & Supply Chain Management*. 8th edition. Harlow: FT Prentice Hall.

For an in-depth academic assessment and critique of Kraljic's model, you should refer to Cox, A. (1997). *Business Success*. Boston, UK: Earlsgate Press and also Cox, A. (2014). *Sourcing Portfolio Analysis* Boston, UK: Earlsgate Press.

Associated models

- Sourcing Gemstone (Model 20)
- Relationship Continuum (Model 21)
- Supplier Preferencing Matrix (Model 23)
- Power-Dependency Model (Model 24)
- Purchasing Chessboard (Model 25)
- Outsourcing Decision Matrix (Model 26)
- Contract Management Grid (Model 31).

MODEL 23
SUPPLIER PREFERENCING MATRIX

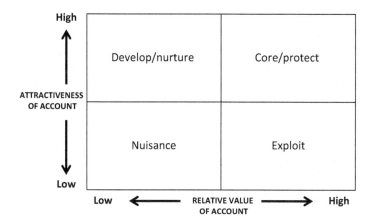

Figure 3.3 Supplier Preferencing Matrix

Source: adapted from Steele and Court (1996).

Overview

Originated by Paul Steele and Brian Court (1996) this model, shown in Figure 3.3, enables procurement functions to understand how a supplier might value its account with them. It suggests that from the supplier's perspective there is a correlation between the attractiveness of the buyer's account and the revenue generation, which in turn affects how the supplier will manage its account with the buyer.

In many ways, the matrix provides a counterview to the Kraljic Matrix (Model 22) in that it is a representation of the supplier's perspective of business.

Elements

The horizontal axis of the matrix is represented by the relative value of the account to the supplier, which serves as a measure of potential revenue. The vertical axis of the matrix represents the attractiveness of the account, which can be quantified in terms of prestige, future business and so on. Each quadrant can be interpreted as follows:

Develop/nurture – These are accounts that bring little in terms of value to a supplier but are very attractive in terms of potential. They are often seen as the supplier's future and much focus is placed on developing this segment of customer relationships.

Core/protect – These are accounts of both high value and attractiveness. They are seen as core business and the supplier places emphasis of levels of service in order to defend their position, while attempting to increase more business.

Nuisance – These are organisations that bring little in terms of value and potential. In this case the supplier might be expected to show little interest or support, and to be actively making efforts to withdraw.

Exploit – These are organisations that may have a high volume of sales, forming substantial revenue, albeit from an account that is not considered to be attractive. In this case, the supplier may concentrate on driving short-term benefits, as retaining the long-term relationship is not considered important.

So what?

This is a useful segmentation model for buyers. It provides a counter-perspective to Kraljic's purchasing portfolio matrix (1983) and can help to explain a supplier's approach towards customer relationship management.

The procurement function can use the outputs from the segmentation exercise to orientate resources and inform decisions in relation to negotiation and supplier relationship management strategies amongst others.

Procurement application

- Assists the development of procurement and category strategies
- Aids both supplier and supply market analysis
- Provides focus to supplier management activities
- Helps to interpret supplier behaviour.

Limitations

One of the obvious limitations of this particular model is that it is predicated totally on guesswork. The buyer is required to make assumptions as to how attractive the account might or might not be, and also what the value of the account is in relation to a supplier's other accounts. From here, the buyer then is expected to use this model to second-guess how the supplier will react.

Some criticism has also been levied at the terms given to the two lower quadrants. The model was developed in the mid-1990s and since this time, greater emphasis has been placed on customer service and account management. Though the model may contain some truisms, the notion that suppliers will treat some customers as a 'nuisance' whilst 'exploiting' others is disingenuous to most modern service-based organisations.

Finally, although billed as a counterview of Kraljic's Matrix, care should be taken when comparing the outputs of these two models. Kraljic's focus is about profiling a category of expenditure, whereas supplier preferencing is about profiling a specific supplier's account management style. The two are very different and should not be automatically cross-referenced.

Further reading

You can read more about supplier preferencing and how it might be applied in:

Steele, P.T. and Court, B.H. (1996). *Profitable Purchasing Strategies.* Singapore: McGraw-Hill.

Associated models

There are several theoretical models related to supplier preferencing, including:

- Boston Box (Model 16)
- Kraljic Matrix (Model 22)
- Power-Dependency Model (Model 24)
- Purchasing Chessboard (Model 25).

MODEL 24
POWER-DEPENDENCY MODEL

	Low	High
High	**B** is dominant over **A**	**A** and **B** are interdependent
Low	**A** and **B** are independent	**A** is dominant over **B**

Relative power of B over A (vertical axis)

Relative power of A over B (horizontal axis)

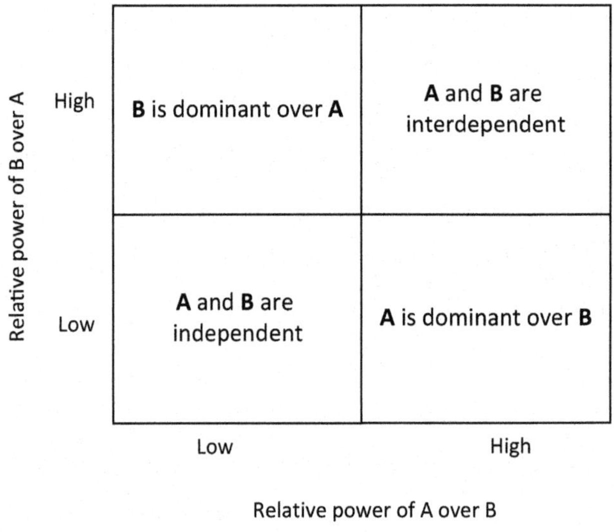

Figure 3.4   Power–Dependency Model

Source: adapted from Cox et al. (2002).

Overview

The Power-Dependency Model shown in Figure 3.4 charts the four potential power structures between any two parties in a commercial relationship. It recognises that both parties have elements that give them power over the other and that therefore these respective positions need to be charted against each other. The authors refer to these elements of power as 'critical assets' but they could equally include intangible assets such as know-how, superior capabilities, market position and/or intellectual property.

The authors of this model claim that the power of one party over another is based on the relative 'scarcity and utility' of each party's resources. For example, a supplier might have access to a specific raw material or a design patent, which gives it relative power over a buyer. Similarly, the buyer might control distribution to a specific market or might have negotiated a restricted covenant on a supplier's business elsewhere.

The model considers the relative strength of each party's power over the other and indicates which of four different power structures apply in any given circumstance.

Elements

B is dominant over A – Party B has dominance because Party A has little or no power over it. Party B can therefore command superior terms. Typically this could occur where a supplier operates a monopolistic market and the buyer has no practical or effective alternative.

A and B are independent – Neither party has any power over the other. This typically might be the case in low value spot purchases within a competitive market. As such, the parties can operate with relative independence to each other.

A is dominant over B – Party A has dominance because Party B has little or no power over it. Party A can therefore command superior terms. Typically this could occur where a supplier is dependent on a buyer for on-going business.

A and B are interdependent – This is the situation where both parties are relatively powerful. For example, there could be contractual lock-in, intellectual property protection, restricted market alternatives and so on. As these scenarios apply to both parties, they become relatively interdependent on each other.

So what?

It is essential for buyers to understand the structure of power in any given supply market or commercial relationship. By understanding this, they are able to determine the most appropriate procurement strategy, negotiation approach and/or commercial terms. Put simply, without understanding the structure of power, a buyer risks being commercially ineffective.

Business relationships are becoming increasingly complex and therefore power dimensions – and more particularly how each party uses them – are important to ensure purchasers are getting the best value for their organisation.

Procurement application

- Analysis of existing supplier relationships and how to manage performance most effectively
- Understanding supply markets prior to sourcing from them
- Helps to construct effective category strategies.

Limitations

The authors of the model provide detailed academic descriptions of different power structures at play. However, they do not provide a succinct definition of 'critical assets' nor do they detail the way in which you can practically determine the relative power between the parties. As a result, although there is a lot of academic validity in the model it remains difficult to apply in practice.

Furthermore, the model fails to inform you what you should do in each of the four situations – and this is an essential omission in its practical application.

Further reading

You can read more about the Power-Dependency Model in:

Cox, A. et al. (2002). *Supply Chains, Markets and Power; Mapping Buyer and Supplier Power Regimes.* London: Routledge.
Cox A. (2014). *Sourcing Portfolio Analysis.* Boston, UK: Earlsgate Press.

Associated models

- Competition Analysis (Model 15)
- Relationship Continuum (Model 21)
- Kraljic Matrix (Model 22)
- Purchasing Chessboard (Model 25).

MODEL 25

PURCHASING CHESSBOARD

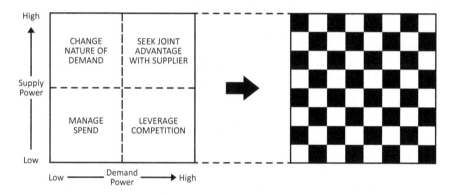

Figure 3.5   Purchasing Chessboard

Source: adapted from Schuh et al. (2008).

Overview

The Purchasing Chessboard was first launched by the consultancy AT Kearney back in 2008 as a tool to derive the best method for reducing costs and increasing value when engaging a supplier (Schuh et al., 2008). Put simply, they claimed to be able to map "supply power" against "demand power" and deliver 64 different purchasing [procurement] strategies for an organisation to pursue.

The premise starts by cross-referencing these power dynamics to create four basic procurement strategies (shown in Figure 3.5) that can be used to support discussions between an organisation's procurement team and its key stakeholders. To this, 16 different levers of value are applied in order to determine the 64 individual strategies.

As a result of this detailed analysis, a 'best fit' strategy can be found to help organisations get better value from their supply-base. The model has proved popular with many large corporates, but not without its criticisms (see for example Cox, 2014).

Elements

The 64 strategies are categorised by their overarching basic strategy as follows:

Manage spend (low demand power/low supply power)

Demand management	Demand reduction
	Compliance management
	Contract management
	Closed loop spend management
Co-sourcing	Procurement outsourcing
	Sourcing community
	Mega-supplier strategy
	Buying consortia
Volume bundling	Bundling across product lines
	Supplier consolidation
	Bundling across sites
	Bundling across generations
Commercial data mining	Master data management
	Cost data mining
	Spend transparency
	Standardisation

Change nature of demand (*low demand power/high supply power*)

Risk management	Bottleneck management
	Vertical integration
	Political framework management
	Intelligent deal structure
Innovation breakthrough	Core cost analysis
	Invention on demand
	Design for sourcing
	Leverage innovation network
Technical data mining	Product benchmark
	Composite benchmark
	Complexity reduction
	Process benchmark
Re-specification	Product teardown
	Functionality assessment
	Design for manufacture
	Specification assessment

Leverage competition (*high demand power/low supply power*)

Globalisation	Global sourcing
	Make or buy
	LCC sourcing
	Bestshoring
Tendering	Supplier market intelligence
	RFI/RFP process
	Reverse auctions
	Expressive bidding
Target pricing	Cost-based price modelling
	Cost regression analysis
	Linear performance pricing
	Factor cost analysis
Supplier pricing review	Price benchmark
	Total cost of ownership
	Unbundled prices
	Leverage market imbalances

Seek joint advantage with supplier (*high demand power/high supply power*)

Integrated operations planning	Visible process organisation
	Collaborative capacity management
	Vendor managed inventory
	Virtual inventory management
Value chain management	Supplier tiering
	Value chain reconfiguration
	Sustainability management
	Revenue sharing
Cost partnership	Supplier development
	Total life cycle concept
	Supplier fitness programme
	Collaborative cost reduction
Value partnership	Project-based partnership
	Profit sharing
	Value-based sourcing
	Strategic alliance

So what?

Procurement managers are regularly challenged with developing a relevant strategy that suits the specific circumstances of the markets they are sourcing from. Rather than develop a 'one-size fits all' approach, the Purchasing Chessboard suggests a 'horses for courses' approach that is contingent on the supply/demand power dynamics.

Although the complexity of 64 different strategies can seem somewhat overwhelming to practitioners, the model demonstrates that there many choices facing procurement managers and suggests that the commercial power dynamics within a market will influence which strategy is most appropriate at any one time.

Procurement application

- Helps to identify suitable procurement strategies
- Provides a framework for creative thought
- Supports the development of a category management plan
- Helps support the development of corporate strategy.

Limitations

Though the Purchasing Chessboard may look sophisticated, serious questions need to be asked about its practical application and rigour. Many of the 64 individual strategies are common sense and completely unrelated to supply and demand power dynamics (for example: demand reduction, contract management, global sourcing, spend transparency, sustainability management and so on). The concept of pinpointing one of these strategies to very specific supply and demand characteristics is far-fetched.

Others have gone a lot further in their criticisms. Professor Andrew Cox (2014) claimed the model lacks coherence by focusing on the supply market as a single entity and not focusing on the power dynamics of individual suppliers within it. He also argues that many of the strategies could equally apply across many of the grid cells within the model, rather than just one – and he is correct.

Further reading

You can read more about Purchasing Chessboard in:

Schuh, C. et al. (2012). *The Purchasing Chessboard*. 2nd edition. London: Springer Science+Business Media, LLC.
Cox, A. (2014). *Sourcing Portfolio Analysis*. Boston, UK: Earlsgate Press.

Associated models

- Sourcing Gemstone (Model 20)
- Kraljic Matrix (Model 22)
- Power-Dependency Model (Model 24).

MODEL 26
OUTSOURCING DECISION MATRIX

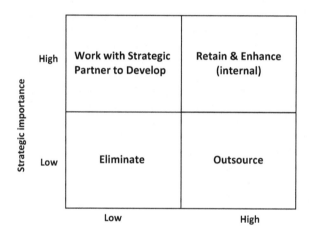

Figure 3.6 Outsourcing Decision Matrix

Source: adapted from Greaver (1999).

Overview

Outsourcing has been a popular theme since the mid-1990s when the concept of organisational core competencies came to the fore. The theory was simple: concentrate on what you do best and pass on the operation of other 'non-core' processes to a third party outsource supplier, who should be better placed to give you higher service levels at lower costs.

Since this time, outsourcing became so popular that many have branded it as another management 'fad' – particularly with a number of notable outsourcing failures being publicised throughout the business world. At one time, it seemed that consulting firms were so eager to outsource that few would consider the risks and consequences involved.

This management model provides a simple decision-making tool for business managers. In essence it neatly sums up the "make vs. buy" business decision, see Figure 3.6.

Elements

The matrix provides four decision outcomes for organisations to manage their business processes effectively depending on the degree of strategic importance and operational performance:

Outsource – The business process delivers high operational importance but is not of high strategic importance to the client organisation. It can therefore be outsourced to a third party with minimal strategic risk.

Retain & enhance – The business process is of such high operational and strategic importance to the client organisation that it must retain the process in-house and work on it to enhance the service delivery. In other words, outsourcing to a third party would be too risky for the organisation.

Eliminate – The business process is of such low strategic and operational importance that the client organisation should either reduce or eliminate it altogether. The challenge here is that if the process is unimportant and of low performance, then why is the organisation doing it at all?

Work with strategic partner to develop – The business process is of high strategic importance and therefore needs to be controlled in-house rather than outsourced. However, due to the low operational performance, a third party 'partner' organisation should be engaged to support and develop the delivery. This also supports the 'buy-in' contracted services approach.

So what?

Many outsourcing activities have brought significant value to organisations in terms of lowering operational costs, enhancing service delivery and releasing working capital. If the right decision is made and the operational processes are carried out properly, then outsourcing can be a major source of competitive advantage.

This model assists the business manager in making the decision of whether to outsource or not. It helps ask the questions and contextualise the business process in the overall strategic agenda of the organisation concerned.

Procurement application

*   Informs the buyer's organisation whether to outsource or not
*   Helps support procurement in its discussions with key stakeholders to influence the 'make vs. buy' decision

- Positions outsourcing as a potential outcome in the strategic decision-making process for managing resources
- Supports the development of effective category strategies.

Limitations

The model provides a solid starting point in the 'make vs. buy' decision process, but should not be considered complete in any way. There will be many theoretical arguments over the differences between what is 'strategic' and 'operational', and what either term really means. There is also the danger that this relatively simple four-box matrix over-simplifies the strategic thinking required to make 'boundary of the firm' decisions.

Those wanting a further in-depth study of outsourcing and outsourcing decision-making are recommended to study the works of Andrew Cox (see below).

Further reading

You can read more about outsourcing decisions in:

Greaver, M.F. (1999). *Strategic Outsourcing: A Structured Approach to Outsourcing Decisions and Initiatives*. New York: Amacom.

Lonsdale, C. and Cox, A. (1998). *Outsourcing: A Business Guide to Risk Management Tools and Techniques*. Boston, UK: Earlsgate Press.

Associated models

- Relationship Continuum (Model 21)
- Kraljic Matrix (Model 22)
- Power-Dependency Model (Model 24)
- Porter's Value Chain (Model 50).

MODEL 27
EARLY SUPPLIER INVOLVEMENT

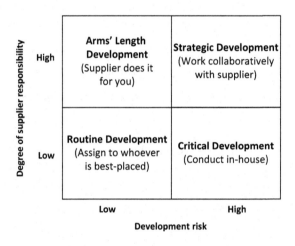

Figure 3.7   Early Supplier Involvement

Source: adapted from Wynstra and Ten Pierick (2000).

Overview

Early Supplier Involvement (ESI) has been described by the Institute of Supply Management as: *"A practice that brings together one or more selected suppliers with a buyer's product design team early in the product development process. The objective is to utilise the supplier's expertise and experience in developing a product specification that is designed for effective and efficient roll-out"*.

The thinking behind the concept is one of joint-working and collaboration between buyer and supplier. In effect, the buyer utilises the supplier's expertise in a particular product or service by involving them in the development of the specification and design. As a result, the end product/service should have better functionality and quality – it may even be more economic too.

Wynstra and Ten Pierick's model (shown in Figure 3.7) allows the buyer to select the most appropriate way in which the supplier should be engaged, depending on how much responsibility the buyer needs the supplier to take and also the degree of risk involved.

Elements

Arms' length development – The development risk is relatively low for the buyer and the supplier needs to take a high level of responsibility in the design process because of its know-how and/or capabilities. An arms' length approach to development is required where *the supplier does it for you*.

Strategic development – The development has many risks attached to it and yet the level of responsibility required from the supplier is also high. A strategic approach to development is required where *the buyer should work collaboratively with the supplier*.

Routine development – The development risk is relatively low and also the degree of supplier responsibility required is relatively low. A routine approach is required where *the development is assigned to whoever is best-placed*.

Critical development – In this situation, the development risk is very high and yet the degree of supplier responsibility required is relatively low. The model suggests that *the development should be conducted in-house by the buyer's organisation*.

So what?

In determining the most appropriate way to involve the supplier in the development process of a new product or service, the buyer is able to utilise the supplier's market and/or technical knowledge in the best way. This allows purchasing to control the risks whilst also harnessing the expertise of third parties.

The model recognises that, at times, involving the supplier is the right thing to do but that, on other occasions, it is best to carry out the design and development in-house. In this way, the model helps inform the buyer how to best engage resources in the market.

Procurement application

- Informs the buyer how best to access supplier capabilities, resources, know-how and expertise
- Can help reduce product lead-time, while also enhancing quality and value
- Allows procurement to get better product and also work collaboratively with the supply chain
- Helps to build effective category strategies.

Limitations

Buyers should not follow the model blindly without assessing the risks in full. ESI can open the buying organisation up to additional risks, such as loss of control on critical information, increased risk of competitive discovery and/or longer lead-times.

It does not always follow that involving suppliers is a good thing – some suppliers can act opportunistically – and so ensuring that there are the appropriate controls in place is essential.

Further reading

You can read more about ESI in:

Lysons, K. and Farrington, B. (2012). *Purchasing & Supply Chain Management*. 8th edition. Harlow: FT Prentice Hall.
Wynstra, F. and Ten Pierick, E. (2000). Management of supplier involvement in new product development. *European Journal of Purchasing and Supply Management*, 6, 49–57.

Associated models

- Product Life Cycle (Model 6)
- Sourcing Gemstone (Model 20)
- Kraljic Matrix (Model 22)
- Outsourcing Decision Matrix (Model 26).

MODEL 28

STAKEHOLDER
MANAGEMENT MATRIX

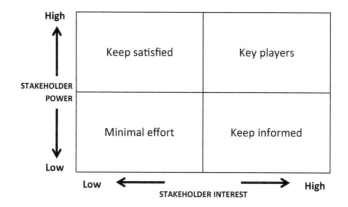

Figure 3.8   Stakeholder Management Matrix

Source: adapted from Mendelow (1991).

Overview

First published in 1991, the model shown in Figure 3.8 looks at understanding the influence that different stakeholders have on strategy development. It does this by classifying the stakeholders in relation to the power they hold and the extent to which they are likely to show an interest in supporting or opposing accordingly.

Elements

Although the power of each stakeholder will vary from industry to industry, market to market and country to country, two key factors will remain the same, namely:

- The interest each stakeholder shows in communicating their expectations on the organisation's strategy
- The levels of power and persuasion the stakeholder possesses to enable this to occur.

The four key elements of the matrix are as follows:

- **Minimal effort (low power/low interest)** – The stakeholders in this group do not require much effort in consultation.
- **Keep informed (low power/high interest)** – These stakeholders need to be kept informed, but mostly as a matter of courtesy, since they have little power.
- **Keep satisfied (low interest/high power)** – The stakeholders need to be kept satisfied because they have high power and they could prove resistant if they were to be upset by your actions.
- **Key players (high interest/high power)** – These are the 'key players', who must be consulted and considered at every stage of change because their active support is needed to get things done. They are likely to have direct influence and responsibility for resources that are needed.

So what?

Understanding stakeholders in this way can enable better and more meaningful communication. For example, continually arranging face-to-face meetings with a stakeholder who has little power could be avoided and thus more focus placed on those that are key decision makers.

The model can be extended beyond just strategy development to be applied to any aspect of procurement delivery.

Procurement application

- Builds a profile of key business stakeholders to the procurement function
- Assists with building cross-functional relationships
- Aids cross-functional communication
- Supports cross-functional development of category management
- Helps to gain support and buy-in to decision making.

Limitations

The matrix provides a simple way of analysing stakeholders; however, once this activity has been performed, it does not help you to understand how to communicate with them appropriately. For this, the work of Daft and Lengel (1998) is recommended.

Further reading

You can read more about stakeholder management and the impact it can have upon developing strategy in:

Johnson, G., Whittington, R., Scholes, K., Angwin, D. and Regner, P. (2010). *Exploring Strategy: Text and Cases.* 11th edition. Harlow: Pearson.

Associated models

- Communication Process (Model 4)
- Rapport Matrix (Model 33)
- Action-Centred Leadership (Model 42).

MODEL 29
JOHARI WINDOW

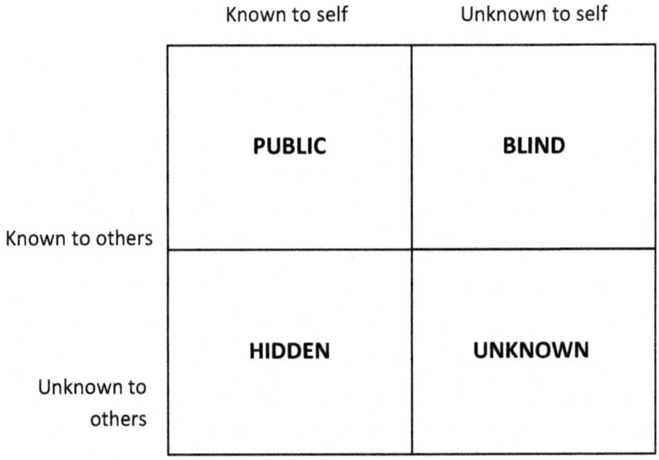

	Known to self	Unknown to self
Known to others	**PUBLIC**	**BLIND**
Unknown to others	**HIDDEN**	**UNKNOWN**

Figure 3.9   Johari Window

Source: adapted from Luft and Ingham (1955).

Overview

The Johari Window shown in Figure 3.9 was developed by American psychologists Joseph Luft and Harry Ingham in 1955. Johari is a combination of their first names (and if you did not know that then you have demonstrated how information can move from the 'blind' quadrant of the Johari Window across to the 'public' quadrant).

The model is widely used as an analysis tool to understand awareness, personal development, interpersonal relationships and group dynamics.

It has become increasingly popular over the last decade due to the emphasis on 'soft skills' in the work place and is sometimes referred to as a 'disclosure/feedback model of self-awareness'.

Elements

The Johari Window is based upon a 2×2 matrix which provides four 'window panes' of information about an individual. The mechanism for populating the model is via a questionnaire containing a list of adjectives which are selected by participants to describe the person in question.

The four window panes are as follows:

Public – Words that are chosen by the individual and his/her peers are placed into this quadrant and represent traits that they are both aware of.

Hidden or façade – Words that are chosen only by the individual are placed into this quadrant. These represent information about him or her that peers are unaware of. It is then the prerogative of the individual as to whether this is disclosed to the others.

Blind spot – Words that are not chosen by the individual but only by peers are placed into this quadrant. These represent information about the individual that he/she is not aware of, but others are. It is then the prerogative of the peers as to whether and how they inform the individual about these 'blind spots'.

Unknown – Words that are not selected by either the individual or his/her peers remain in the 'unknown' quadrant. This represents the individual's behaviours or motives that were not recognised by anyone, because either they have not been exhibited or because there is a collective ignorance of their existence.

It should be noted that the ultimate goal of the model is to enlarge the 'public' area without disclosing information that is too personal. To this end, panes can be correspondingly changed in size to reflect the amount of information received.

So what?

The Johari Window provides a visual reference that individuals can use to look at their own character and to develop from. It also illustrates the importance of sharing, being open and accepting feedback from others.

Performed properly the process can facilitate discussion and build trust within groups, and is often used within team development scenarios.

Procurement application

- Can form part of a training needs analysis programme
- Feedback can be incorporated with performance development reviews
- Useful tool for building trust and openness within teams
- Sometimes used within SRM programmes to facilitate sharing and openness.

Limitations

Because of the model's simplicity and hence popularity, it has been copied and borrowed by other academics over the years and consequently terminology surrounding the framework has become muddled – for example Charles Handy (2000) referred to the model as the 'Johari House' with 'four rooms'.

It is also recognised that problems can occur during implementation of the model as the definition of 'self-disclosure' can vary tremendously and often there are issues with the amount of information actually revealed by the individual at the centre of the exercise.

Finally, it should also be remembered that the effectiveness of a 360° feedback process often relies upon the experience and sensitivity of those managing it. An important factor to consider when working internationally, as some cultures can interpret constructive criticism as offensive.

Further reading

You can read more about self-awareness analysis and Luft and Ingham's theories in:

Luft, J. and Ingham, H. (1955). The Johari Window: a graphic model of interpersonal awareness. *Proceedings of the Western Training Laboratory in Group Development.* Los Angeles, CA: UCLA.

And also Handy's interpretation in:

Handy, C. (2000). *21 Ideas for Managers.* San Francisco, CA: Jossey-Bass.

Associated models

- Situational Leadership (Model 41)
- Tuckman Model (Model 43)
- Innovation Diffusion (Model 53).

MODEL 30
SUPPLIER
CATEGORISATION

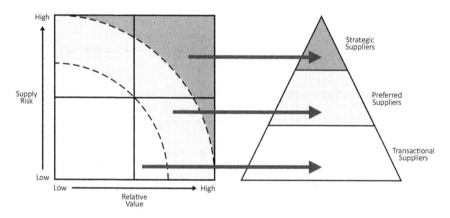

Figure 3.10   Supplier Categorisation

Overview

Supplier Categorisation is a technique most associated with supplier relationship management (SRM). It represents a segmentation process for identifying and prioritising the highest value third-party supplier relationships, so that additional collaboration (and leverage) can be applied to extract added-value and innovation from the commercial relationship.

Typically most medium-sized and large organisations have hundreds, if not thousands of third-party contracts with suppliers and they need a model like Supplier Categorisation to identify those that contain the highest value. This model is based on a simple adaptation and extension of the Kraljic Matrix (Model 22). It is perhaps the most common and popular of all supplier segmentation models currently in existence.

Elements

Relationship segmentation is based upon an evaluation of the associated risk and value within each supplier relationship. There are three tiers within the Supplier Categorisation model:

Strategic suppliers	• Relationships of 'strategic' value
	• Top-tier, highest value, most critical suppliers
	• Usually <5% (by number), often <1%
	• Targeted relationships for joint-working and collaboration
	• Relationships that generate added-value, continuous improvement and innovation
	• Often characterised by mutual dependency and 'co-destiny'.
Preferred suppliers	• Relationships based on preferential trading terms
	• Mid-tier, mid-value, 'important' suppliers
	• Usually 20–30% (by number)
	• Relationships that require performance management and will generate a degree of continuous improvement
	• Often characterised by long-term contracts and contract management activities.
Transactional suppliers	• Short-term relationships based on standard terms
	• Lowest-tier, low value, low risk contracts
	• Predominantly a contractual exchange with limited extent of 'relationship'
	• Trading relationship that simply requires the minimum regulatory monitoring
	• Characterised by contracted and transactional terms.

So what?

Managing supplier relationships is immensely time and resource consuming, with the benefits often only being realised over a long time horizon (at least 3+ years). Many large organisations with significant spend have commenced SRM activities only to find that they fail to yield the benefits purported by consultants.

The Supplier Categorisation model helps organisations to segment their supply-base and identify key suppliers that could be targeted for SRM. These relationships should be only the highest value/highest risk relationships where there is a degree of criticality in the relationship that justifies the added investment of SRM. Here (in the top-tier) 'strategic suppliers' are collaborated with over the longer-term so that there is a close-working mutually-beneficial relationship that delivers added tangible value for both sides.

Once the Supplier Categorisation model has been used to identify and target these top suppliers, SRM activities and a joint-working supplier development programme can commence.

Procurement application

- Segments the supply-base and identifies 'strategic suppliers'
- Prioritises SRM activities
- Supports the business case for supplier development programmes.

Limitations

Whilst being one of the most popular supplier segmentation models, Supplier Categorisation is based on a simplistic portfolio methodology (such as that devised by Kraljic, 1983) and is therefore fraught with risks and assumptions. For a fuller discussion on this you should refer to the Kraljic Matrix (Model 22) or authors such as Cox (2014). The model is based on limited parameters and characterised solely by the buyer's perspective of the relationship, rather than a two-way shared understanding of the relationship dynamics. Put simply, what is 'strategic' for one party is automatically [and wrongly] assumed to be 'strategic' to the other.

Similarly, the Supplier Categorisation model fails to account for the structures of power (and dependency) within supply chain relationships. Using this as a SRM segmentation tool assumes that high spend and high risk relationships will automatically create relationships of shared inter-dependency (i.e. with both parties sharing a degree of power and leverage over the other). However, this is rarely the case in real-life. In this regard, a better segmentation model would be an adaptation of Cox's Power-Dependency Model (Model 24) such as that developed by Vitasek (2011) in her 'business mapping framework'.

Supplier Categorisation has been adapted and developed by a number of other authors and consultants. For example, O'Brien (2017) has introduced a "Help, Hurt, Heroes" assessment to his SRM approach which then segments into a pyramid with four tiers of supplier relationship (strategic, important ongoing, important short-term and non-important). Although this gives the appearance of extra layers of sophistication, it does little to address the underlying limitations in the model.

Further reading

You can read more about the process of Supplier Categorisation in either of the following three publications, although none specifically details the more commonly used model detailed within this chapter:

Booth, C. (2010). *Strategic Procurement: Organizing Suppliers & Supply Chains for Competitive Advantage*. London: Kogan Page.
O'Brien, J. (2017). *The Buyer's Toolkit*. London: Kogan Page.
Vitasek, K. et al. (2011). *The Vested Outsourcing Manual*. New York: Palgrave Macmillan.

Associated models

- Relationship Continuum (Model 21)
- Kraljic Matrix (Model 22)
- Supply Preferencing Matrix (Model 23)
- Power-Dependency Model (Model 24)
- Contract Management Grid (Model 31).

MODEL 31
CONTRACT MANAGEMENT GRID

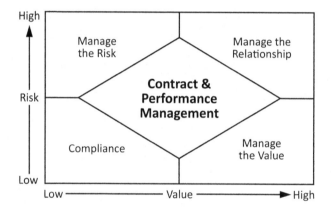

Figure 3.11   Contract Management Grid

Overview

The Contract Management Grid has been used by various public bodies over the last few years as a segmentation tool to identify the type of contract management that is required for various contracts. The model is based on a variant of the Kraljic Matrix (Model 22) and therefore takes on the buyer's perspective of the risk and value associated with any one individual contract.

The grid allows an organisation to identify its highest risk and highest value contracts and nominate specific contract managers for each of them. It also highlights the purpose and emphasis of any contract management activities (i.e. by demonstrating what the contract manager needs to focus on when delivering through the contract).

The grid shown in Figure 3.11 is the authors' adaptation of the original four-box matrix developed by Graham Collins of ProQuest Consulting on behalf of

Buckinghamshire County Council, which has been produced with permission but has not been previously published.

Elements

There are five main elements to the Contract Management Grid based on an analysis of a contract's risk and value:

Compliance	Low risk/low value contracts:
	• Typically at least 50% of an organisation's contracts are in this category
	• The focus should be on satisfying the minimum regulatory requirements but little else
Manage the risk	High risk/low value contracts:
	• These represent high risk contracts where there is vulnerability and exposure
	• The contract manager needs to prioritise risk management and mitigation activities proactively
Manage the value	Low risk/high value contracts:
	• Typically up to 40% of an organisation's spend is in this category
	• The contract manager needs to prioritise cost and value management on a proactive basis
	• The greatest opportunities for cost reduction and quality improvement are here
Manage the relationship	High risk/high value contracts:
	• Typically less than 5% of an organisation's contracts are in this category
	• A significant amount of proactive contract management and supplier relationship management (SRM) is required
	• Both value and risk need to be equally managed in collaboration with the supplier
Contract & performance management	Medium risk/medium value contracts:
	• Typically at least 30% of an organisation's contracts fall into this mid-point
	• The contract management team needs to focus on the general performance on the contract

So what?

Most medium-sized and large organisations have hundreds or thousands of third-party contracts and so it impossible to expect each and every contract to be managed in the same manner with the same level of resource and management effort. The Contract Management Grid helps organisations to prioritise their contracts around the dimensions of risk and value. Those of higher value and/or risk need to be prioritised over the others and this tool will help achieve that.

By plotting each and every contract on the model, organisations can identify specific contracts that need more proactive attention. The model also helps to determine the focus of the contract management team (i.e. to focus on managing/mitigating value or on managing/extracting added-value – or both).

As authors, we have worked closely with client organisations who have taken thousands of contracts through this segmentation tool and subsequently set up improvement plans for clusters of contracts. This is a valuable method of proactively applying contract management principles.

Procurement application

- Prioritises activities for contract management teams
- Helps to set performance improvement targets
- Helps targets key risk mitigation opportunities
- Helps target key value improvement opportunities.

Limitations

The Contract Management Grid is a great starting place for organisations looking to develop a proactive contract management discipline, however it is just a starting place. As with its progenitor (the Kraljic Matrix, Model 22), this model is based solely on the buyer's perspective of the contract. In other words, it is one-dimensional and overlooks the supplier's perspective. Similarly, some might also argue that this model fails to analyse the underlying structures of power within a contract and is therefore short-sighted and suboptimal.

Another criticism of this model is that it does not go far enough to instruct the user exactly what they should be doing to manage a contract in any of these matrix quadrants. Determining that a contract needs to 'manage risk' or 'manage value' is relatively superficial and uninformative.

Our final criticism of the model is the central diamond panel: "contract & performance management". If the model is used to segment an organisation's full suite of third-party contracts there is a major risk that a significant number will end up being 'dumped' in this middle section by default. Protagonists of this model may argue this is a good thing, thereby segmenting out the contracts only of the highest risk and/or highest value. However, it could leave users extremely frustrated that their segmentation exercise has just left up to 70% of contracts in one somewhat 'nebulous' category.

Associated models

- Contract Management Cycle (Model 2)
- Kraljic Matrix (Model 22)
- Supplier Categorisation (Model 30).

SECTION 4

Negotiation

MODEL 32
THE NEGOTIATION PROCESS

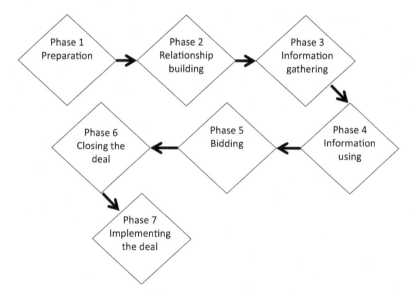

Figure 4.1   The Negotiation Process
Source: adapted from Greenhalgh (2001).

Overview

It is generally accepted that there are several key phases within a typical negotiation process. Professor Leonard Greenhalgh published his version in 2001 and it has been widely used as a basis for other similar models since then.

The model shown in Figure 4.1 identifies the basic 'process' of negotiation in a linear series of sequential steps.

Elements

This model is particularly relevant for integrative negotiations and outlines seven key steps to an 'ideal' negotiation process:

1. **Preparation** – Deciding what is important, defining goals, thinking ahead how to work together with the other party.
2. **Relationship building** – Getting to know the other party, understanding how you and the other are similar or different, building commitment toward achieving a mutually beneficial set of outcomes.
3. **Information gathering** – Learning what you need to know about the issues, the other party and their needs, the feasibility of potential settlements, and what might happen if you fail to reach agreement with the other side.
4. **Information using** – At this stage, negotiators assemble the case they want to make for their preferred outcomes and settlement, one that will maximise the negotiator's own needs. This presentation is often used to 'sell' the negotiator's preferred outcome to the other.
5. **Bidding** – The process of making moves from one's initial, ideal position to the actual outcome. Bidding is the process by which each party states their "opening offer", and then makes moves in that offer toward a middle ground.
6. **Closing the deal** – The objective here is to build commitment to the agreement achieved in the previous phase. Both the negotiator and the other party have to assure themselves that they reached a deal they can be happy with or, at least, live with.
7. **Implementing the deal** – Determining who needs to do what once the agreement is formalised. Not uncommonly parties discover that the agreement has anomalies, key points were missed, or the situation has changed and is sometimes subject to re-negotiation.

So what?

Understanding the natural phases that a negotiation passes through is essential for planning and preparing for a negotiation. Typically this might include considerations such as resource availability, information requirements, individual needs, research and analysis, preparation, targets, opening statements, timing and so on.

Without an agreed process, a negotiation risks drifting and not necessarily fulfilling one's intended outcomes.

Procurement application

*   Supports the negotiation planning and preparation stages
*   Helps identify and create negotiation leverage
*   Aids selection of an appropriate negotiation strategy.

Limitations

This model illustrates the general flow of negotiations over time and assumes an integrative approach. Some of the key phases could be reduced or even eliminated if a distributive approach is taken, for example 'relationship building'.

It should be remembered that negotiation is more than a linear process and will often need adaptation to a particular context or circumstance. Negotiators should be wary of over-reliance on process-based methodologies: negotiation is an art-form that requires embedded skills within the people who lead it.

Further reading

You can read more about the phases of negotiation and their impact in:

Cordell, A. (2018). *The Negotiation Handbook*. 2nd edition. Oxon: Routledge.
Greenhalgh, L. (2001). *Managing Strategic Relationships, the Key to Business Success*. New York: Simon and Schuster Adult Publishing Group.

Associated models

- Rapport Matrix (Model 33)
- Persuasion Tools Model (Model 34)
- Zone of Potential Agreement (Model 35)
- Thomas–Kilmann Conflict Mode Instrument (Model 37).

MODEL 33
RAPPORT MATRIX

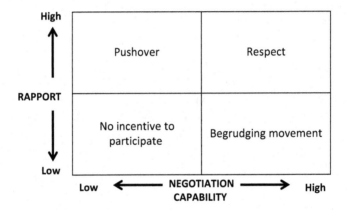

Figure 4.2   Rapport Matrix
Source: adapted from Reynolds (2003).

Overview

The Rapport Matrix shown in Figure 4.2 serves to highlight the importance of combining hard and soft skills when managing stakeholders and conducting negotiations. It considers the need to develop rapport with the other party and consequently establish a relationship within which influencing can be effectively conducted.

Elements

The matrix is based on the skill-base of an individual to create rapport and negotiate respectively. The four quadrants are described as follows:

Pushover – An individual with effective rapport building skills and yet under-developed negotiation capabilities is most likely to be an ineffective negotiator – in essence, a nice person but also a 'pushover' in terms of achieving outcomes.

Respect – The combination of negotiation effectiveness and the ability to develop rapport with others earns respect from others. This enables collaborative and/or strategic negotiations to be executed more effectively.

No incentive to participate – inability to create rapport, combined with low negotiation capabilities, can create significant engagement issues for someone wanting to negotiate. They lack the skills required to develop relationships and also to influence others – and therefore give the impression of not participating in the key issues in need of negotiation.

Begrudging movement – This is the classic 'bear-trap' where negotiators focus so intently on their negotiation prowess, they overlook the need to develop rapport and relationship with others. A deal may be able to be brokered and forced through, but resentment and/or adversarialism could accompany the negotiation and have an adverse effect later in the deal.

So what?

The Rapport Matrix provides an excellent illustration of the importance of soft skills within the context of negotiation. It highlights the need for rapport as an important precursor to relationship building and ultimately to the achievement of an effective and successful negotiated outcome.

Procurement application

- Supports negotiations
- Useful for developing leadership, influencing and negotiation skills
- Helps support supplier relationship management activities where high levels of influencing and persuasion are required.

Limitations

The model is a good *aide memoire* to help remind purchasers of the importance of rapport and relationship when negotiating. However, in itself, the model does not tell individuals how they should develop rapport or what skills are required to achieve it. To understand these dimensions of the model, further study of Reynolds' (2003) work is required.

Further reading

You can read more about the Rapport Matrix and the development of rapport in:

Cordell, A. (2018). *The Negotiation Handbook*. 2nd edition. Oxon: Routledge.
Reynolds, A. (2003). *Emotional Intelligence and Negotiation*. Hampshire: Tommo Press.

Associated models

- Persuasion Tools Model (Model 34)
- Zone of Potential Agreement (Model 35)
- SPIN® Negotiation (Model 39).

MODEL 34
PERSUASION TOOLS MODEL

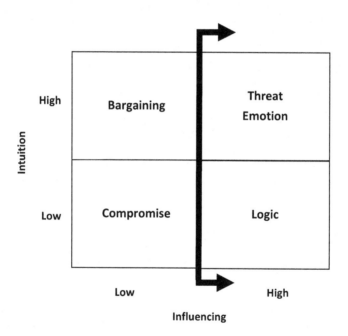

Figure 4.3   Persuasion Tools Model
Source: adapted from Reynolds (2003).

Overview

The Persuasion Tools Model shown in Figure 4.3 was developed by Andrea Reynolds (2003) and is based on Kenneth Berrian's (1944) original work to identify the five widely recognised tools of persuasion. Reynolds has adapted this work and, through empirical research, has linked persuasion styles to emotional intelligence – and in particular the elements of intuition and influencing.

This model is useful for identifying the preferred persuasion approach in oneself and others. Those who tend towards the tools in the top right hand quadrant are thought to be the most effective negotiators.

Elements

The horizontal axis of the matrix is represented by influencing, which serves as a measure of overall persuasion capability. The vertical axis of the matrix represents the level of intuition required when adopting a certain negotiation style. Each quadrant should therefore be interpreted as follows:

Threat/emotion – High levels of both intuitiveness and influencing ability are needed in order to deploy Threat and Emotion appropriately during a negotiation. It is likely that the individuals adopting such styles will be both highly skilled and experienced.

Logic – A powerful tool based on the use of facts and data; therefore, a high degree of intuition is not required. Individuals adopting this style will need to be very articulate and detailed if they are to achieve a successful outcome.

Bargaining – High degrees of influencing capability are not necessarily required to use one of the easiest and most popular methods of negotiation. However, the need to understand when to instinctively use this tool is critical as bargaining at the wrong time (e.g. too soon) could be costly.

Compromise – This is the least powerful and confrontational tool, it requires the least experience and is therefore often favoured by less skilled negotiators.

So what?

It has long been thought that an additional intelligence exists alongside IQ and this has now been recognised as the Emotional Quotient (EQ). Theorists suggest that in order to be successful individuals need both their IQ and their EQ to be higher than average.

Research has shown that chief executives rate influencing and intuition as key factors of career success. This view has led to increased EQ assessment amongst senior managers and it has been found to be particularly helpful in identifying leadership potential.

Procurement application

* Supports negotiations
* Useful for developing leadership, influencing and negotiation skills
* Helps support supplier relationship management activities where high levels of influencing and persuasion are required.

Limitations

The model has been well researched and is supported by empirical data. However, it does not tell you what you need to do to change persuasion styles or how to develop one's negotiation skills beyond this initial assessment. For that, you need to read more on the subject of emotional intelligence.

Berrian's (1944) work on the five main persuasion tools has been used by several consulting firms and writers to suggest that this is their own work. This is not the case – Kenneth Berrian is the originator of this work in his studies of applied psychology during the Second World War and the immediate years that followed.

Further reading

You can read more about persuasion tools and the Persuasion Tools Model in:

Cordell, A. (2018). *The Negotiation Handbook*. 2nd edition. Oxon: Routledge.
Reynolds, A. (2003). *Emotional Intelligence and Negotiation*. Hampshire: Tommo Press.
Berrien, F.K. (1944). *Practical Psychology*. New York: Macmillan.

Associated models

- Rapport Matrix (Model 33)
- Zone of Potential Agreement (Model 35)
- Thomas–Kilmann Conflict Mode Instrument (Model 37).

MODEL 35
ZONE OF POTENTIAL AGREEMENT

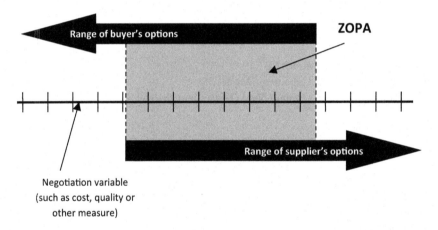

Figure 4.4   ZOPA

Source: adapted from Harvard Business School.

Overview

Initially this model shown in Figure 4.4 was used as a tool for dispute resolution and often associated with the BATNA negotiation approach (best alternative to a negotiated agreement – Fisher and Ury, 1981). The Zone of Potential Agreement (ZOPA) describes the area where agreement may be met between two parties.

ZOPA is about setting targets of a negotiation and minimum 'fall-back' positions. The limits of ZOPA represent each party's fall-back position below which either party would 'walk-away'. Therefore, it is suggested that once both sides have moved into their respective zones (i.e. beyond the fall-back), then it is more probable that consensus will be reached.

Elements

To initiate this process an opening offer needs to be made by one of the parties. This in turn will be evaluated by the receiving party who will take a decision whether to respond or not, and if so in which zone. This will continue until the ZOPA is reached and an acceptable agreement is formulated within the zone.

The range of options just outside the ZOPA is as follows:

Reasonable zone – Considered as the precursor to the ZOPA. It is thought that an opening offer in this region is reasonable enough to be able to move towards a mutually acceptable agreement.

Credible zone – An opening offer here may be perceived as slightly unreasonable and therefore may or may not set a parameter for negotiation.

Extreme zone – An offer opened in this zone will not usually set the parameter for negotiation; however, those offers that are deemed *'extreme but credible'* may trigger movement.

Insult zone – Considered so unreasonable that it not only fails to set the parameter for negotiation, but it may also cause the other party to refuse to continue discussions.

So what?

The ZOPA demonstrates the various positions that can be taken when attempting to reach agreement. This can provide a platform for offer and concession in order to obtain a mutually acceptable resolution.

When establishing a fall-back position, it is important to remember to develop a package of variables in order to create a bargaining mix with which to negotiate. It is also necessary to identify those variables that are 'throwaways' and those that are 'trade-offs', so that concessions can be elicited from the other party who may place more value on them.

Procurement application

- Useful planning tool to create a negotiation strategy
- Supports commercial negotiations and contractual disputes.

Limitations

This model does not take into account the relative strengths, power or interests of the parties, all of which can have an effect upon the process. It also ignores the impact of new information gleaned during the course of an agreement, which can either enhance or limit a party's ability to respond.

The model is predicated on the principal persuasion tools of bargaining and compromise – the weakest forms of negotiation.

Finally, critics have suggested that this model fails to allow for creativity (i.e. through the joint exploration of issues), because each party's fall-back position is already predetermined.

Further reading

You can read more about ZOPA in:

Cordell, A. (2018). *The Negotiation Handbook*. 2nd edition. Oxon: Routledge.

Lax, D.A. and Sebenius, J.K. (1986). *The Manager as Negotiator: Bargaining for Cooperation and Competitive Gain*. New York: The Free Press.

Lewicki, R.J., Saunders, D. and Barry, B. (2009). *Negotiation*. 6th edition. Burr Ridge, IL: McGraw Hill.

Associated models

- The Negotiation Process (Model 32)
- Rapport Matrix (section 4, model 33)
- Persuasion Tools Model (Model 34)
- Thomas–Kilmann Conflict Mode Instrument (Model 37).

MODEL 36
BATNA

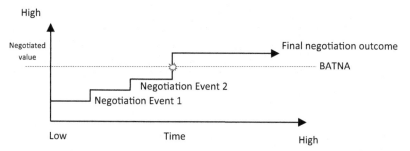

Figure 4.5 BATNA

Source: Cordell (2018).

Overview

BATNA is an acronym for "Best Alternative To a Negotiated Agreement" and was first coined by negotiation researchers Roger Fisher and William Ury (1981) who worked on the Harvard Negotiation Project.

The BATNA as demonstrated in Figure 4.5 is akin to the negotiator's fall-back [contingency] position. However, whereas the term fall-back infers that the agreement reached may be sub-optimal, the BATNA is viewed as an equally good *alternative* to reaching a mutually acceptable settlement. The basic premise is that a negotiator should not accept a worse resolution than their BATNA.

Similarly the BATNA should not be confused with the walkaway point, which suggests that the negotiation cannot reach a successful conclusion (and therefore acts as a trigger for the next best alternative).

Elements

Know your BATNA	It is important to know the point at which you can say no to an unfavourable proposal. A strong BATNA may determine a more advantageous outcome, whereas a weak BATNA could put you in a less favourable position.
Improving your BATNA	You may wish to improve your BATNA by creating more alternatives, thus increasing your power in the negotiation.
Disclose your BATNA	At some stage during the negotiation process it may be beneficial to disclose your BATNA i.e. naming alternative sources of supply.
Consider the other side's BATNA	Knowledge of the other side's BATNA is another source of negotiation strength. Being able to ascertain their position in comparison with your own could provide you with a considerable advantage, especially if you can find a way of weakening their alternative.
BATNA-less	*'The BATNA-less party is a deal taker, not a deal maker'*. Theorists suggest that if you find yourself in this position you should immediately create a BATNA.

So what?

Being BATNA-less means that you are more likely to accept a deal rather than nego-tiate it. Therefore, determining a strong yet flexible BATNA is the key to a successful outcome. However, how do you know if you have set the BATNA correctly? Some academics suggest the following process:

1. Brainstorm a range of alternative options in the event that negotiation fail to reach agreement
2. Choose the most promising and expand them into practical and attainable goals
3. Assess the strength of the options, i.e. strong/weak, as this will help you to decide whether they should be revealed to the other side
4. Rank the options in order to determine your 'Prime BATNA'.

The willingness of a negotiator to break off a negotiation (invoking the BATNA) will allow them to adopt a firmer stance during the bidding phase of the negotiation process – in essence delivering the threat of walking away.

Procurement application

- Planning the negotiation strategy (integrative/distributive)
- Preparing opening statements
- Establishing targets and ranges
- Post-negotiation evaluation.

Limitations

Developed in the early 1980s, the BATNA theory appears to split academics. Many argue that it is more suited to industrial relations negotiations, whereas others promote it as a negotiation fundamental. A concept that has been gathering momentum is that of EATNA – "Estimated Alternative To a Negotiated Agreement". This allows for the many instances where negotiators believe they have a powerful alternative when in actual fact they do not.

Further reading

You can read more about BATNA in:

Cordell, A. (2018). *The Negotiation Handbook.* 2nd edition. Oxon: Routledge.
Fisher, R. and Ury, W.L. (1981). *Getting to Yes: Negotiating Agreement without Giving In.* Boston, MA: Houghton Mifflin.

Associated models

- The Negotiation Process (Model 32)
- Persuasion Tools Model (Model 34)
- Zone of Potential Agreement (Model 35)
- Thomas–Kilmann Conflict Mode Instrument (Model 37).

MODEL 37

THOMAS–KILMANN CONFLICT MODE INSTRUMENT

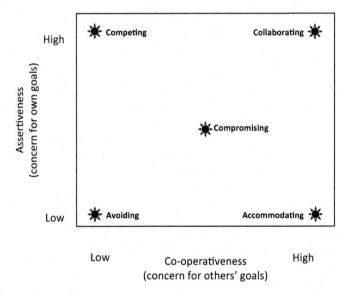

Figure 4.6 Thomas–Kilmann Conflict Mode Instrument

Source: adapted from Ruble and Thomas (1976).

Overview

Initially conceived by Kenneth Thomas in the mid 1970s, he later joined forces with Ralph Kilmann and together they developed the Thomas–Kilmann Conflict Mode Instrument from which the above model shown in Figure 4.6 is a derivative.

The model looks at the five main ways of dealing with conflict in terms of assessing an individual's desire to achieve their goals compared with that of the other party.

Elements

There are five main modes of conflict: Collaborating, Competing, Accommodating, Compromising and Avoiding. Conflict style is assessed by measuring one's assertiveness in relation to one's co-operativeness, as follows:

Collaborating – Assertive and cooperative, the goal is to work with other people in order to establish a win–win solution. This style is often adopted when integrating solutions, gaining commitment or improving relationships.

Competing – Assertive and un-cooperative, the goal is to win. This style is often adopted when quick action and unpopular decisions are required or when there is leverage present.

Accommodating – Unassertive and cooperative, the goal is to yield. This style is often adopted when showing reasonableness, developing performance and creating good will.

Compromising – Occupying the middle position, the goal is to find the middle ground and is often referred to as the 'let's make a deal' mode.

Avoiding – Unassertive and un-cooperative, the goal is to delay. This style is often adopted in order to deal with issues of little importance, to reduce tension or to buy time.

So what?

This is a well-recognised conflict profiling tool, which can aid awareness of individual style as well as provide a selection of alternative methods of engagement (in other words the recognition of response will enable an adaptation of one's personal style to take place).

It is believed that the key to the successful utilisation of this approach to conflict is personal awareness, as failure to recognise one's own or others' styles could result in unsatisfactory resolution.

The modes of conflict resolution can be extended to consider negotiation strategies and styles (Smith, 1987) or even management styles (Blake and Mouton, 1985).

Procurement application

• Supports the preparation for a negotiation with a supplier
• Aids stakeholder management and communication
• Facilitates team meetings and the development of collaborative dynamics.

Limitations

This model assumes that individuals will be capable of switching between the various different styles depending upon the situation. However, human nature is such that in practice there is a habitual tendency to use only a limited number of them, and therefore success is limited to these.

From a negotiation perspective, it has also been argued that the 'compromise' style is merely a replication of 'accommodation', since both are reliant upon concession rather than assertion in order to move forward.

Further reading

You can read more about conflict theory and the work of Kenneth Thomas in:

Buchanan, D. and Huczynski, A. (2010). *Organizational Behaviour.* 7th edition. Harlow: Pearson.
Cordell, A. (2018). *The Negotiation Handbook.* 2nd edition. Oxon: Routledge.

Associated models

- Rapport Matrix (Model 33)
- Persuasion Tools Model (Model 34)
- Zone of Potential Agreement (Model 35)
- Managerial Grid (Model 46).

MODEL 38
SALES POSITIONING
MATRIX

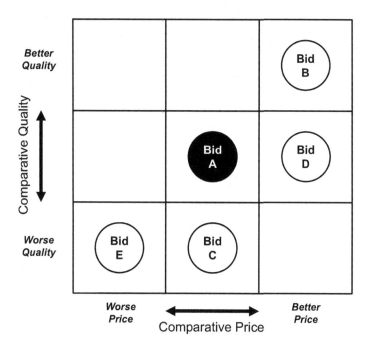

Figure 4.7 Sales Positioning Matrix

Overview

The Sales Positioning Matrix is used as a negotiation preparation tool once an initial offer has been made by a seller. This is a comparative model that helps negotiators understand the relative strengths of weaknesses on one specific offer in comparison with competing bids.

As authors, we first came across the model shown in Figure 4.7 when working with the global sales team for one of our clients and, taking the underlying concept, we adapted it to suit the procurement profession. The model helps to understand some of the processes sales professionals go through when preparing to defend a tender or quotation that they have submitted to their client – but of course it suits the buyer's position so much more effectively, not least of all because the buyer has full insight to the relative strengths and weaknesses of all of the bids it has received during a sourcing exercise.

As procurement professionals, we can use this matrix to highlight the relative merits of competitive bids and to prepare a negotiation strategy. Sales professionals can use the same model to prepare a defence of their offers, based on their current understanding of the market.

Elements

The Sales Positioning Matrix maps the relative merits of a bid on two key competing dimensions: price and quality. By positioning the selected offer in the central quadrant, all competing bids are plotted around the centre to highlight whether their prices and/or quality are better, the same or worse than the bid in question. The comparative price is easy to understand (providing all bids have been priced on a comparative basis) but in this context quality has a broad definition, referring to all of the non-price elements in an offer (i.e. functionality, service, quality, scope, etc).

The model shown in Figure 4.7 indicates five competing bids:

Bid A	Bid A is the offer that is being compared with all others. It represents the supplier that is about to be negotiated with so that an improved offer can be received from them.
Bid B	This position represents an alternative offer that is superior to Bid A in terms of both price and quality. Bid A will therefore need to be improved on both accounts if it is to compete on a parity basis with Bid B, as indicated by the arrow.
Bid C	This position represents an offer that is of the same price but lower overall quality than Bid A. The supplier of Bid A may well be aware they are offering superior quality and so the buyer needs to focus on improving price during the negotiation.
Bid D	This position represents an offer that is of lower price but equivalent quality to Bid A. When negotiating with the supplier of Bid A, the buyer needs to focus on how the quality offering can be improved to differentiate the bids, given that the price of Bid A is already better.
Bid E	This position represents an offer that is worse in terms of both price and quality than Bid A. If Bid A already has all of the required elements that the buyer is seeking, then it can afford to discount Bid E.

So what?

In a simple visual snapshot, the buyer is able to plot the comparative positions of competing offers mid-way through a sourcing exercise. This is particularly useful for post-bid negotiations, where the buying team needs a strategy to improve the offers it has received in order to get the best overall value from the sourcing exercise.

The model depicts which bids are better and on what grounds. It provides a simple graphical comparison to shown stakeholders and to ensure the negotiation team is aligned on its objectives.

For the sales side (where this model first originated) the model can be used to 'position' the seller's offering vis-à-vis its market rivals. It requires a strong understanding of the competition, but becomes a useful market analysis tool to defend an opening offer to a customer.

Procurement application

- Supports bid evaluation during a competitive sourcing exercise
- Helps to prepare a negotiation strategy
- Visual tool for communicating with stakeholders.

Limitations

Though the Sales Positioning Matrix is a useful addition to the procurement professional's toolkit, it is not a panacea. Firstly, it is patently obvious that the bid comparison is only two-dimensional when most bids nowadays have many more factors to consider. Quality has been treated as a single component of the analysis, when in fact is an aggregation of several features – some of which will be more significant than others.

Secondly, the model is not instructive; it does not tell buyers what they should be doing or how to negotiate with the seller – it is purely a comparison. This could be a source of frustration for the buyer, as it merely reinforces that one bid is better than another.

Associated models

- SWOT Analysis (Model 17)
- Kraljic Matrix (Model 22)
- Supplier Preferencing Matrix (Model 23)
- BATNA (Model 36).

MODEL 39
SPIN® NEGOTIATION

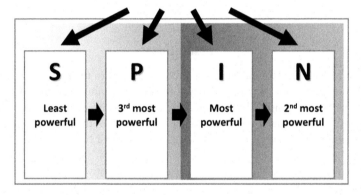

Question-based techniques for Consultative Selling

S — Least powerful
P — 3rd most powerful
I — Most powerful
N — 2nd most powerful

Figure 4.8   SPIN® Negotiation

Source: adapted from Rackham (1995).

Overview

SPIN® refers to a commonly used sales negotiation technique founded in the late 1980s by Neil Rackham (1995).It is based on a questioning process that highlights the sequential steps to be followed when trying to make a sale (see Figure 4.8).

This model is useful for influencing and is seen as a consultative rather than aggressively overt sales technique. It focuses on developing a need in the buyer's mind and then selling them a solution in order to meet it.

Elements

The four steps in the process each have a defined outcome, which needs to be met before proceeding to the next stage. Failure at any one of them can result in an ineffective sales attempt.

Situation – These questions are designed to establish the client's existing situation. They should be asked economically, as it is believed that this is the least powerful position in the process and that effort could be more usefully directed elsewhere.

Problem questions – These questions are designed to find out more about potential problems that may exist in the current situation. This is thought to be the third most powerful step in the process and normally provides the basis for the sale.

Implication – These questions involve implying that there is a need for a solution to the problems highlighted. It is believed that this is the most powerful stage as it is about implanting a need for the solution in the customer's head.

Need/payoff – These questions are about helping the customer to articulate the benefits of finding a solution to the problem, and then proposing a solution which meets their needs. This is deemed to be the second most powerful step in the process.

So what?

This model is most commonly used by sales professionals and is regarded as one of the best techniques for persuading buyers to part with their money. Based on research by Huthwaite Inc, one of the leading sales training organisations, it is widely regarded as a tried and tested sales tool.

It has also grown in popularity as a consultancy tool where clients are provided with solutions after problems have been diagnosed.

Procurement application

- Supports negotiations
- Helps internal client engagement
- Helps buyers to understand how suppliers' salespeople and account management teams are trained.

Limitations

The SPIN® process is predicated on the sequential steps being followed together with a level of expertise that is capable of eliciting the desired outcome. One of the main barriers to success is that there is a natural tendency to spend too much time exploring the issues initially, leaving insufficient time to close the deal.

Although the consulting company behind the use of this model (Huthwaite) will point to a plethora of empirical evidence supporting the success of SPIN®, questions must be raised about the competence of the buyer (professional or otherwise) and the structure of power in the dyadic buyer–seller relationship that leads to a salesperson taking control of the sales meeting through question-based selling. Most professional purchasers would not tolerate this and most professional sourcing processes could not accommodate this approach. Therefore, the model is probably best suited for informal sales meetings with non-professional buyers.

Further reading

You can read more about Rackham's selling technique in:

Rackham, N. (1995). *SPIN® Selling*. Hampshire: Gower.

Associated models

- Rapport Matrix (Model 33).
- Persuasion Tools Model (Model 34)
- Zone of Potential Agreement (Model 35)
- Thomas–Kilmann Conflict Mode Instrument (Model 37).

SECTION 5

Management

MODEL 40

CONTINUUM OF
LEADERSHIP BEHAVIOUR

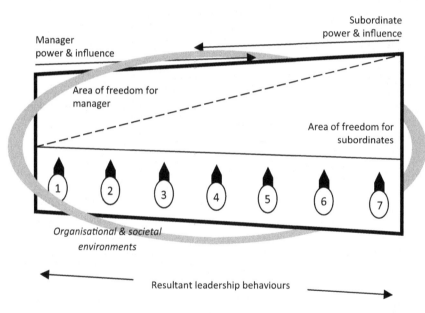

Figure 5.1   Continuum of Leadership Behaviour

Source: adapted from Tannenbaum and Schmidt (1973).

Overview

Lewin, Lippitt and White (1939) were the first academics to suggest that there were three different leadership approaches – *autocratic, democratic* and *laissez-faire*. This theory was further developed by Robert Tannenbaum and Warren Schmidt (1973), who published their initial model in 1958. This model, shown in Figure 5.1, called the 'continuum of leadership behaviour' describes the range of possible leadership styles available to managers. This was later updated in 1973 to reflect a number of organisational and societal changes.

Elements

The behaviours adopted should reflect three forces at work:

- Forces in the manager, such as personality, preferences and beliefs
- Forces in the subordinates, such as the need for independence and expectations of involvement
- Forces in the situation, such as organisational norms, size, location and time pressure.

The seven types of leadership behaviour have the following characteristics:

1. **Manager makes a decision and announces it** – Only the manager plays the decision-making role; there is no subordinate involvement
2. **Manager "sells" decision** – No change in decision; but subordinates may raise some concerns
3. **Manager presents ideas and invites questions** – Subordinates know what options the manager considered for the decision; some subordinate involvement
4. **Manager presents tentative decision subject to change** – Subordinates can have a say on manager's decision; it can be changed based on discussion
5. **Manager presents problem, gets suggestions, makes decision** – Subordinates are free to come up with options; manager decides on those options
6. **Manager defines limits, asks group to make decision** – Manager delegates to subordinates; but still manager is accountable for the outcome
7. **Manager permits subordinates to function within limits defined by superior** – Complete freedom level; team does all the work almost as well as the manager does.

So what?

The main advantage of this model for leaders and managers is that it defines the criteria for involvement and delegation when dealing with subordinates. In parallel it can also highlight subordinates' development and empowerment needs.

Procurement application

- Useful diagnostic tool for managers and leaders in the procurement function
- Increases awareness of alternative leadership behaviours
- Can be used to support performance reviews.

Limitations

Academics criticise the theory because it assumes that the leader/manager has sufficient information to determine the disposition of both self and team, and also that it assumes the environment is "neutral" (i.e. without social bonds or politics).

It also been suggested that the model simplifies complex decisions to a bi-polar dimension, which is more simple than reality.

Further reading

You can read more about Tannenbaum and Schmidt and their Continuum of Leadership Behaviour theory in:

Boddy, D. (2016). *Management: An Introduction.* 7th edition. Harlow: Pearson.

Lewin, K., Lippit, R. and White, R.K. (1939). Patterns of aggressive behavior in experimentally created social climates. *Journal of Social Psychology*, 10, 271–301.

Tannenbaum, R. and Schmidt, W.H. (1973). How to choose a leadership pattern. *Harvard Business Review*, May/June.

Associated models

- Situational Leadership (Model 41)
- Managerial Grid (Model 46).

MODEL 41
SITUATIONAL LEADERSHIP

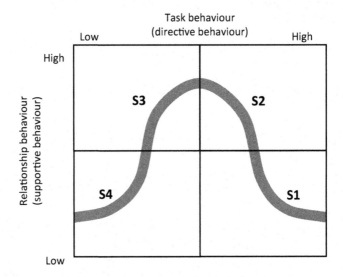

Figure 5.2   Situational Leadership

Source: adapted from Hersey (1984).

Overview

First published by Paul Hersey and Kenneth Blanchard (1974), the Situational Leadership approach is probably the most popular formal model of leadership behaviour. The authors suggest that managers must adopt different leadership styles depending on the 'readiness' level of the individual to be led.

The model shown in Figure 5.2 correlates an individual's readiness (represented by the stages R1, R2, R3 and R4) against the different styles of leadership required (represented by the styles S1, S2, S3 and S4) – thus allowing a manager to determine which style of leadership most appropriately suits the given situation, i.e. the 'situational' approach.

Elements

The leadership styles are defined in terms of task behaviour (the amount of direction given) and relationship behaviour (the amount of facilitation and support provided):

Style of Leadership
S1 "Telling" – Above average amounts of task behaviour and below average amounts of relationship behaviour
S2 "Selling" – Above average amounts of both task and relationship behaviour
S3 "Participating" – Above average amounts of relationship behaviour and below average amounts of task behaviour
S4 "Delegating" – Below average amounts of both relationship behaviour and task behaviour.

The readiness of an individual is defined in terms ability (knowledge, experience and skill) and willingness (confidence, commitment and motivation):

Individual's Attitude and Ability
R1 Low Readiness – Unable and unwilling or insecure
R2 Low to moderate Readiness – Unable but willing or motivated
R3 Moderate to high Readiness – Able but unwilling or insecure
R4 High Readiness – Able and willing or motivated.

So what?

Hersey and Blanchard's (1974) Situational Leadership model can be used either when choosing how to respond to a given situation involving an individual or when developing a team.

It should be remembered that regardless of the level of readiness of an individual or group, change may occur. In particular, when performance begins to slip and/or ability or motivation decreases, the leader should reassess the readiness level and move backward through the leadership curve, providing the appropriate socio-emotional support and direction.

Procurement application

- Useful diagnostic tool for managers and leaders in the procurement function
- Determines the most appropriate style of leadership for the given situation
- Can be used to support performance reviews.

Limitations

This model is often criticised for failing to distinguish between management and leadership, as many of the requisite behaviours could be more closely associated with that of management as opposed to leadership. On this basis, some theorists believe the model should be entitled 'situational management'.

It has also been argued that the model places too much emphasis on what the leader does rather than the individual and, therefore, mis-positioning on the matrix could occur.

Further reading

You can read more about Hersey and Blanchard's Situational Leadership approaches in:

Hersey, P., Blanchard, K. and Johnson, D.E. (2001). *Management of Organizational Behavior.* 8th edition. Upper Saddle River, NJ: Prentice Hall.
Mullins, L. (2016). *Management and Organisational Behaviour.* 11th edition. Harlow: Pearson.

Associated models

- Continuum of Leadership Behaviour (Model 40)
- Managerial Grid (Model 46).

MODEL 42
ACTION-CENTRED
LEADERSHIP

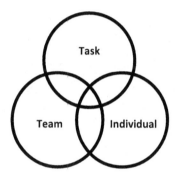

Figure 5.3 Action-Centred Leadership

Source: adapted from Adair (1979).

Overview

John Adair (1979) started to develop his Action-Centred Leadership model shown in Figure 5.3 while lecturing at Sandhurst Royal Military Academy during the 1960s. Adair was one of the first theorists to suggest that leadership is a trainable and transferable skill, rather than it being an exclusively inborn ability.

The three parts of Adair's model are commonly represented by three overlapping circles, which have become one of the most recognisable symbols within management theory.

Elements

The three main elements of the model overlap in order to suggest each can have an impact upon the other. If one element is missing or under-developed, then the others will suffer. Therefore, leaders should concentrate on all three as follows:

Achieving the task – which can involve identifying aims and vision, purpose and direction, resources, creating the plan, establishing responsibilities, creating standards, monitoring performance and reporting progress.

Developing the individual – which can include understanding the team members, supporting and mentoring, agreeing individual responsibilities and objectives, giving recognition and training and development.

Building and maintaining the team – which can mean establishing, agreeing and communicating standards of performance and behaviour, developing a culture, resolving conflict, identifying and agreeing team objectives.

So what?

This simple model is often seen as a 'blueprint' for leadership and the management of any team, group or organisation. It is independent of situation or organisational culture and enables a leader to identify where he or she may be losing touch with the real needs of the group or situation.

Procurement application

- Useful diagnostic tool for managers and leaders in the procurement function
- Increases awareness of key leadership objectives
- Acts as a useful reminder for leaders on how to balance their time and resources effectively.

Limitations

Critics have claimed that Adair's approach has now become outdated given the pace and scale of changes in the work environment during the last 20 years. Akin to this is the view that the model takes little account of flatter structures that are now generally preferred as the most effective organisational form.

Some academics have also denounced Action-Centred Leadership as being too 'authoritarian', applicable in a rigid, formal, military-type environment, but less relevant to the modern workplace, where the leadership emphasis is on leading change, empowering, enabling, managing knowledge and fostering innovation.

Arguably, the model also takes little account of stakeholders or the increasingly 'networked' matrix of the modern organisation.

Further reading

You can read more about John Adair and Action-Centred Leadership in:

Adair, J. (1979). *Action-Centred Leadership*. London: Gower Publishing.
Boddy, D. (2016). *Management: An Introduction*. 7th edition. Harlow: Pearson.
Mullins, L. (2016). *Management and Organisational Behaviour*. 11th edition. Harlow: Pearson.

Associated models

- Continuum of Leadership Behaviour (Model 40)
- Situational Leadership (Model 41).

MODEL 43
TUCKMAN MODEL

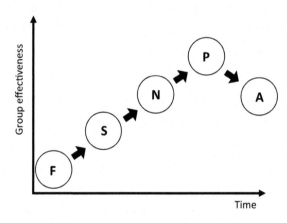

Figure 5.4   Stages of Team Development

Source: adapted from Tuckman and Jensen (1977).

Overview

The team development model was first published by Dr Bruce Tuckman (1965). He subsequently added the 'Adjourning' stage in 1977 in conjunction with Mary-Ann Jensen (Tuckman and Jensen, 1977) to create the model shown in Figure 5.4.

Tuckman's theory suggests that all teams go through a chronological order of stages in terms of development and accompanying behaviour.

Elements

The order of progression is as follows:

1. **Forming** – Individuals come together as a group for the first time with a common purpose or goal. This is the information gathering stage, where individuals are creating roles for themselves.
2. **Storming** – Differences and conflicts become apparent. If the group cannot overcome these, then it may not be able to move past this stage.
3. **Norming** – If the team members overcome the previous stage, they will start actively working together and accommodating different methods and norms. Individuals will begin to fully understand the purpose of the group and the role they play in it.
4. **Performing** – Not all groups reach this stage. If they do then they are performing to a high standard and in an efficient manner. Roles and responsibilities change according to need and there is a strong sense of group identity.
5. **Adjourning** – This is about completion and disengagement both in terms of tasks and group members. It is believed that a sense of mourning is experienced as the group identity is dissolved.

So what?

This model helps newly formed teams to understand how they might become effective, acknowledging that different behaviours will be exhibited throughout development. More latterly, Blanchard, Carew and Carew (2004) identified the leadership requirements of each stage of the process.

Procurement application

*   Develops understanding of team dynamics both functionally and with stakeholders
*   Aids project management when working with cross-functional procurement teams
*   Assists conflict resolution.

Limitations

Tuckman's original work was purely a descriptive observation of how groups evolve. In reality the value of the model comes from identifying which stage a particular group may be, and then supporting it through to the performing stage.

Further reading

You can read more about Tuckman and team development in:

Blanchard, K., Carew, D. and Pandarisi-Carew, E. (2004). *The One Minute Manager Builds High Performing Teams* (The One Minute Manager). London: HarperCollins Publishers.
Boddy, D. (2016). *Management: An Introduction.* 7th edition. Harlow: Pearson.
Mullins, L. (2016). *Management and Organisational Behaviour.* 11th edition. Harlow: Pearson.
Tuckman, B.W. and Jensen, M.A.C. (1977). Stages of a small-group development revisited. *Group & Organization Studies,* 2, 419–427.

Associated models

- Thomas–Kilmann Conflict Mode Instrument (Model 37)
- Situational Leadership (Model 41).

MODEL 44
THE BALANCED SCORECARD

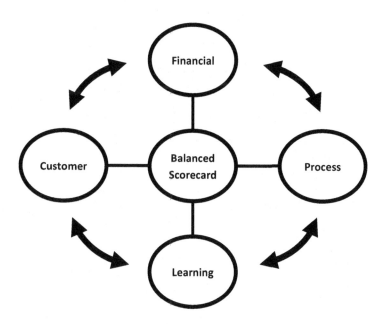

Figure 5.5 The Balanced Scorecard

Source: adapted from Kaplan and Norton (1996).

Overview

Originated by Drs. Robert Kaplan and David Norton (1996), the Balanced Scorecard shown in Figure 5.5 is a planning and management system that is used to align business activities to the vision and strategy of an organisation. It combines non-financial measures with traditional financial metrics to give managers a more 'balanced' view of organisational performance.

Elements

The Balanced Scorecard provides a clear prescription as to what organisations should measure in order to 'balance' the financial perspective with other non-financial metrics:

Learning – Includes employee training and corporate cultural attitudes related to both individual and corporate self-improvement, ease of communication as well as technological tools, such as an intranet or learning management system.

Process – These metrics show how a business is running and whether its products and services conform to customer requirements (the 'mission').

Customer – Measures customer satisfaction and focus. Can be an indicator of future trends/decline, even though the overall financial position of the organisation is good.

Financial – Traditional metrics that should be timely and accurate. Additional financially-related data such as risk assessment and cost-benefit information could also be included.

So what?

Performance measures or indicators are measurable characteristics of products, services, processes and operations that an organisation can use to track and improve performance.

The integration of the four perspectives into a graphical picture has made the Balanced Scorecard a very successful methodology within value-based management philosophy. According to the authors, the chief executive can use a Balanced Scorecard in monitoring the operating performance of an organisation much like a pilot uses a dashboard to fly a plane.

Procurement application

- Helps develop 'balanced' metrics for a procurement team, project or function
- Supports procurement marketing activities across the organisation – not just financial savings
- Effective communication tool of the performance across a team, project or function.

Limitations

Overall the Balanced Scorecard is a framework for cross-functional measurement. It is easy to use, but very general in nature. It does not tell you what you should measure – or how you should measure – and therefore has obvious limitations, other than being a set of good practice principles for adoption into a wide variety of contexts.

Some academics argue that the model does not place sufficient focus on quality and consequently other models, such as *The Performance Prism*, have been developed.

Further reading

You can read more about the Balanced Scorecard and how it can be applied to various organisational contexts in:

Kaplan, R.S. and Norton, D.P. (1996). *The Balanced Scorecard: Translating Strategy into Action*. Boston, MA: HBS Press.

Lysons, K. and Farrington, B. (2012). *Purchasing & Supply Chain Management*. 8th edition. Harlow: FT Prentice Hall.

Associated models

•   The Iron Triangle (Model 45).

MODEL 45
THE IRON TRIANGLE

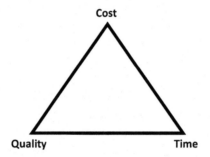

Figure 5.6 The Iron Triangle

Overview

The Iron Triangle shown in Figure 5.6 is a project management model that dates back to the late 1960s and 1970s, where major capital investment projects came under increasing pressure to use resources effectively. The principle is that the apexes (cost, quality and time) form the basic delivery requirements of any project and that they are mutually interdependent.

Thus, should a procurement manager place pressure on a project to reduce cost or improve quality, there will be a 'knock on' consequential effect on the other parameters. In effect, the triangle sides become rigidly connected, such that changing one of these project requirements has a direct impact on at least one of the others.

Elements

The three elements of the Iron Triangle (sometimes referred to as 'constraints') are explained below:

Cost – Relates to all commercial elements of a project, including total cost, rate of return, project yield and return on investment, etc.

Quality – Relates to all quality aspects such as specification, scope, materials, tolerances and performance, etc.

Time – Relates to all aspects of the project timescales, including lead time, float, critical path and delivery deadlines, etc.

The implication of the Iron Triangle is that an improvement in one element can only be achieved at the expense of at least one (if not both) of the other elements.

The model is also commonly referred to as the 'triple constraints' of project management, or sometimes just the 'project management triangle'.

So what?

The Iron Triangle refers to a principle for managing projects. This is not only for major capital investment projects, it could simply refer to organisational initiatives such as a sourcing exercise or any other procurement initiative.

The 'iron triangle' is a good tool to help remember that each of the elements of cost, quality and time are interrelated – it applies just as equally to the delivery of goods and services from a supplier, as to that of projects.

Ultimately, it means that should a manager wish to improve one of the elements, there will be 'trade-offs' with the other two.

Procurement application

• Useful model to remember the inter-connected variables of procurement activities

• Good practice project management principle that applies just as much to the supply of goods and services from a supplier, as it does major projects.

Limitations

The Iron Triangle is a 'truism' – it is fairly obvious that if you want to improve the delivery time on something, then there will be potential cost or quality implications.

Modern thinking has started to challenge the convention of the Iron Triangle. There are now several 'landmark' projects where cost, quality and time improvements have all been achieved without the consequential compromises suggested by this model. Techniques such as value engineering and business process reengineering help managers to challenge these preconceptions and therefore deliver the type of results that 'best practice' projects now require.

Further reading

You can read more about the Iron Triangle in:

Goldratt, E.M. (1990). *What Is This Thing Called Theory of Constraints and How Should It Be Implemented?* Great Barrington, MA: North River Press.
Maylor, H. (2010). *Project Management.* 4th edition. Harlow: FT Prentice Hall.

Associated models

- The Balanced Scorecard (Model 44).

MODEL 46
MANAGERIAL GRID

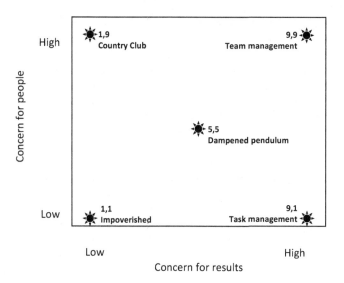

Figure 5.7   The Managerial Grid

Source: adapted from Blake and Mouton (1985).

Overview

Originally published by Blake and Mouton in 1962, the Managerial Grid in Figure 5.7 plots an individual's style of management in terms of their relative concern for people versus concern for results. This can be assessed via a diagnostic questionnaire and subsequently plotted on a 9 × 9 grid.

151

Elements

There is an assumption that individuals gravitate towards a natural management style and that this can be classified in terms of the balance between people and task issues. The Y axis – 'concern for people' – is the degree of interest in people's needs and feelings, whilst the X axis – 'concern for results' – is the degree of interest in tasks such as resources, procedures and results.

The managerial styles on the grid are as follows:

Country Club management – Suggests that good relations are key but that there is minimal concern for the achievement of work-based results.

Team management – Both people and work issues are of equal concern and these are both managed well.

Impoverished management – There is little concern for either people or work activities.

Task management – Sometimes referred to as 'produce-or-peril' or 'authority-compliance'. In this position, the concern for work activities is high, but there is little interest in people.

Dampened pendulum – Often referred to as 'middle of the road' management, where concern for both people and work issues is relatively equal and 'sufficient'.

So what?

Arguably, effective managers need to ensure that they balance their time and resources on managing both the task and the people involved in equal measure.

In general terms, a manager that becomes either overly task-oriented or overly people-oriented risks being ineffective.

The Blake and Mouton Managerial Grid allows a degree of personal assessment of management styles so that the individual can be aware and, if need be, compensate for their naturally preferred style.

Procurement application

- Useful diagnostic tool for managers and leaders within a procurement function
- Increases awareness of personal management styles
- Can be used to support personal development planning and/or training needs analysis.

Limitations

The Managerial Grid does not consider situational circumstances, as it is based on a one-person/one-style approach. For example, country club management may be the most effective style with a group of experts or self-motivated people, whereas task management may be the best approach in a situation where staff have a low desire for independence, even during a crisis. The model does not consider that an effective manager is able to adapt his or her style as appropriate.

Further reading

You can read more about Blake and Mouton and the Managerial Grid in:

Blake, R.R., Mouton, J.S. and Bidwell, A.C. (1962). The Managerial Grid. *Advanced Management – Office Executive*, 1(9), 12–15.

Blake, R.R. and Mouton, J.S. (1964). *The Managerial Grid*. Houston, TX: Gulf Publishing.

Blake, R.R. and Mouton, J.S. (1985). *The Managerial Grid III: A New Look at the Classic That Has Boosted Productivity and Profits for Thousands of Corporations Worldwide*. Houston, TX: Gulf Publishing Co.

Mullins, L.J. (2016). *Management & Organisational Behaviour*. 11th edition. Harlow: Pearson.

Associated models

- Continuum of Leadership Behaviour (Model 40)
- Situational Leadership (Model 41).

MODEL 47

MASLOW'S HIERARCHY OF NEEDS

Figure 5.8   Maslow's Hierarchy of Needs

Source: adapted from Maslow (1943).

Overview

Abraham Maslow originally published his theory of individual development and motivation in 1943. His basic proposition was that people are 'wanting' beings who constantly desire more, and that these 'wants' are dependent on what they already have.

Maslow's Hierarchy of Needs (Figure 5.8) is usually shown as a tiered range operating through five main levels, starting at the lowest level and working through each level to fulfil the top level of 'self-actualisation'.

The theory suggests that gaining more of the same does not provide motivation and that, in order to provide motivation for change, managers must direct their attention to the next higher level of need.

Elements

The hierarchy of needs is mainly displayed in the form of a pyramid, which implies a thinning out of needs as people progress up the hierarchy.

There are five main stages within Maslow's model, starting at the lowest level:

Physiological needs – These are basic needs required such as food, water, oxygen and sleep.

Safety needs – These needs include safety and security and also include the need for predictability, orderliness and protection from danger or deprivation.

Love needs – These can sometimes be referred to as social needs and are the need for affection, friendships, social activities and a sense of belonging and the giving and receiving of love.

Esteem needs – These include both self-respect (involving the desire for strength, independence, achievement, freedom and confidence) as well as esteem from others (involving reputation, status, attention, appreciation and recognition).

Self-actualisation needs – The highest level in Maslow's Hierarchy of Needs. Once reached, the person will have developed and realised their full potential in following their personal beliefs and values.

So what?

This is a useful framework for motivation theory and it is helpful for managers to consider the needs and motivations of their staff and colleagues. The theory has stood the test of time and provides the basis for several other related motivational theories.

At its heart, the model recognises that all individuals are motivated by self-interest but that the drivers will evolve as the individual progresses.

The model can also be extended beyond a leadership application to consider the motivations of customers and suppliers from a relationship management perspective.

Procurement application

Aside of the obvious (another leadership model that applies to leadership position in a procurement function) there are other procurement related applications.

One of the most common adaptations of the Hierarchy of Needs principles has been in the area of business requirements analysis. The concept is based on the prioritisation of organisational needs for a purchase. These might include: regulatory, assurance of supply, service, quality, cost and/or innovation. Every purchase can have these basic needs applied to them and prioritised accordingly as part of the stakeholder engagement process that procurement would go through prior to the development of a specification. Accordingly, through consultation, stakeholders can decide which of the business requirements take priority over others (for example cost vs. quality). The outputs then translate to the basis of a specification and the contract award criteria.

Limitations

Models that claim to map out the behaviour and motivations of individuals will always be limited at best. Each individual will have a different requirement to the next and what may fulfil one person may not be the same for the other. Although Maslow's hierarchy is relatively universal there are differences in an individual's motivation dependent on their culture.

Further reading

There are numerous books about Maslow's Hierarchy of Needs, but we suggest you refer to any of the following:

Buchanan, D. and Huczynski, A. (2016). *Organizational Behaviour.* 9th edition. Harlow: Pearson
Maslow, A.H. Stephens, D.C. and Heil, G. (1998). *Maslow on Management.* New York: John Wiley & Sons Inc.
Mullins, L. (2016). *Management and Organisation Behaviour.* 11th edition. Harlow: Pearson

Associated models

- Action-Centred Leadership (Model 42)
- Thomas–Kilmann Conflict Mode Instrument (Model 37).

SECTION 6

Organisation

MODEL 48
MCKINSEY 7S FRAMEWORK

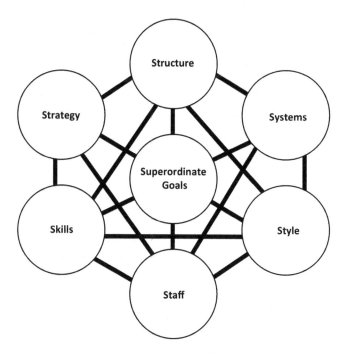

Figure 6.1   McKinsey 7S Framework

Source: adapted from Peters and Waterman (1982).

Overview

The 7S Framework was developed by Tom Peters and Robert Waterman (1982) and then taken up as a strategy tool by the global management consultancy company

McKinsey & Company.

This model shows seven essential interconnected factors that influence an organisation's effectiveness, especially its ability for strategic change.

The framework suggests that to implement effective change at the strategic level, you need to impact all seven factors – not just one in isolation.

Elements

The framework has no obvious starting point as all of the elements are equally important. They are also interconnected; therefore changing one may well impact on others. The elements are as follows:

Strategy – The direction of the company from a long-term perspective in order to obtain a competitive advantage.

Structure – The organisation of the company and the levels of responsibility amongst employees.

Systems – The procedures, processes and routines that characterise how the work should be done, such as financial systems and recruiting.

Superordinate goals – The collective vision, 'values' and culture of the company and its employees.

Skills – The combination of core competencies of both employees and the organisation as a whole.

Staff – The company's employees, including their work ethic, procedures and training and development.

Style – The general operating style of the company and the mode of leadership used.

So what?

This framework is commonly used as a strategic 'auditing' tool in order to identify organisational resources and the importance of the links between them.

Procurement application

* Supports the procurement planning process in terms of assessing resources
* Aids supplier analysis
* Acts as a check list of important factors when considering change within the procurement environment.

Limitations

The framework shows the relationships that exist but it provides limited clues as to what constitutes more effective strategy and implementation.

It has also been criticised for ignoring areas such as innovation, knowledge, customer driven service and quality, all of which have subsequently been identified as being important in relation to corporate strategy development.

Further reading

You can read more about the McKinsey 7S Framework in:

Peters, T. and Waterman, R. (1982). *In Search of Excellence*. USA: Warner Books.
Lynch, R. (2018). *Strategic Management*. 8th edition. Harlow: Pearson.

Associated models

- Ishikawa's Fishbone Diagram (Model 8)
- Strategy Development (PCA Model) (Model 12)
- Cultural Web (Model 49)
- Force Field Analysis (Model 51).

MODEL 49
CULTURAL WEB

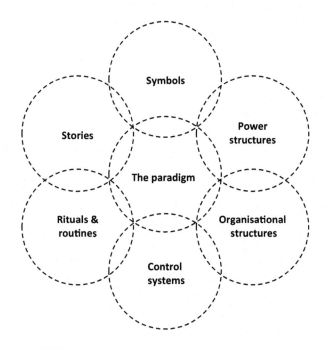

Figure 6.2   Cultural Web

Source: adapted from Johnson (1987).

Overview

Developed by Gerry Johnson (1987), the Cultural Web shown in Figure 6.2 is a useful model that brings together the basic elements required to analyse the culture of an organisation.

The assumption is that the paradigm that develops from these is central to the ongoing 'heartbeat' of the organisation.

Elements

The paradigm at the centre of the model comprises the combined key beliefs and assumptions of the organisation. This is impacted to varying degrees by the following:

Stories – This indicates the stories and general portrait of the organisation as demonstrated by its employees.

Symbols – Typified by branding and corporate logos, it also includes inherent attributes such as office layout and the language and terminology adopted by staff.

Rituals & routines – This is the fundamental culture of the organisation including recognition and reward, training, disciplinary procedures and working patterns.

Power structures – This correlates to the grouping and levels of power within the organisation, such reward mechanisms and/or delegated authorities.

Control systems – This refers to performance measurement and review processes, as well as policies and procedures.

Organisational structures – This is the formal hierarchy – the chain of command within an organisation.

So what?

The Cultural Web can help to distinguish between what is done officially in an organisation, such as press releases and post-project evaluation, and what is done unofficially, such as grapevine stories, office parties, e-mail messages and so on.

The resulting paradigm links the elements but may also tend to preserve them as 'the way we do things here'.

Procurement application

- Assists with the assessment of an organisation's (or function's) culture
- Supports the procurement planning process
- Aids supplier appraisal, in terms of cultural fit.

Limitations

The model has been criticised for ignoring the possibility that several cultures could exist within an organisation at the same time. This correspondingly could impact upon the pace of change in relation to any proposed strategy implementation, for example one part of the organisation may be more readily accepting than others.

Further reading

You can read more about the Cultural Web in:

Johnson, G., Whittington, R., Scholes, K., Angwin, D. and Regner, P. (2017). *Exploring Strategy: Text and Cases.* 11th edition. Harlow: Pearson.

Johnson, G. (1987). *Strategic Change and the Management Process (Corporate Strategy, Organization & Change).* Hoboken, NJ: Wiley-Blackwell.

Associated models

- Strategy Development (PCA Model) (Model 12)
- SWOT Analysis (Model 17)
- The Balanced Scorecard (Model 44)
- McKinsey 7S Framework (Model 48).

MODEL 50
PORTER'S VALUE CHAIN

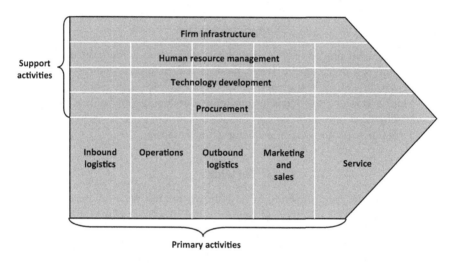

Figure 6.3   Porter's Value Chain

Adapted from: Porter (1985).

Overview

Popularised by Michael Porter (1985), the Value Chain shown in Figure 6.3 categorises the generic value-adding activities within an organisation. Porter argued that it is necessary to examine them separately in order to identify where competitive advantage may exist.

The Value Chain can also be used to demonstrate where cost is added – and thus highlight the relative balance between added-value and cost within a function.

Porter's Value Chain is an internal examination of activities and should not be confused with the supply chain concept of value chains.

Elements

The Value Chain is made up of two types of activities: primary and support. Primary activities are those which are directly involved with the output of the product, whereas support activities are those which improve the primary activities:

Primary activities:

- Inbound logistics: receiving, storing and distributing
- Operations: transforming inputs into products
- Outbound logistics: collecting, storing and delivering the product or service to the customer
- Marketing and sales: consumer awareness of the product or service and where they can purchase it
- Service: after sales support.

Support activities:

- Procurement: process of obtaining the necessary inputs for the primary activities
- Technology development: R&D, product and/or process improvements, (re) design, developing new services
- Human resource management: obtaining, developing and training employees within the company
- Firm infrastructure: systems and setup of the company.

So what?

Porter's model helps organisations to focus on where most value can be added to an organisation. Strategic planners and consultants use it extensively to map out a company's strengths and shortcomings.

It is often used when analysing strategic alliances and merger and acquisition deals in order to get to get a quick overview of the possible match.

The Value Chain can also be used to identify areas that are non-value-adding, which are potential targets for outsourcing to a more economic service provider.

Porter also stated that the value chain of several organisations within a supply chain could be analysed to identify where the value-adding activities are within a supply chain – he referred to this as the 'value network'.

Procurement application

- Supports supplier analysis when developing a sourcing strategy
- Builds overall business awareness of one's own organisation and thus increases credibility with internal stakeholders
- Helps to develop functional strategies by identifying value-adding (or non-value-adding) activities.

Limitations

In practice this model is extremely difficult to operationalise. An in-depth analysis of an organisation's cost-base and internal financing arrangements goes beyond most organisation's capabilities.

In 1985, when Porter introduced the Value Chain, around 60% of most Western economies' workforces were active in manufacturing industries. Nowadays, most service industries in Western countries employ over 80% of the workforce. As a result, critique on the Value Chain model and its applicability to services organisations has since been voiced by both academics and practitioners.

Further reading

You can read more about Porter's Value Chain in:

Porter, M.E. (1985). *Competitive Advantage: Creating and Sustaining Superior Performance.* New York: The Free Press.

Johnson, G., Whittington, R., Scholes, K., Angwin, D. and Regner, P. (2017). *Exploring Strategy: Text and Cases.* 11th edition. Harlow: Pearson.

Associated models

- Strategy Development (PCA Model) (Model 12)
- SWOT Analysis (Model 17)
- Outsourcing Decision Matrix (Model 26).

MODEL 51
FORCE FIELD ANALYSIS

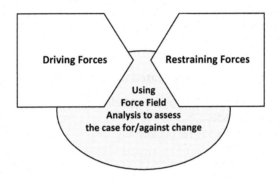

Figure 6.4   Force Field Analysis

Source: adapted from Lewin (1947).

Overview

Kurt Lewin (1947) developed the concept of the Force Field Analysis after observing group dynamics at work. It is a useful model for managers who need to plan and execute change management in their organisation.

Force Field Analysis helps managers to predict the likely response to proposed changes and identify where the greatest resistance may come from. The diagram shown in Figure 6.4 helps to map the forces driving and restraining the proposed change.

Elements

Force Field Analysis suggests that in every social system there are *Driving Forces* trying to change the current situation and *Restraining Forces* trying to prevent that change taking place. Some examples are shown below:

Examples of *Driving Forces* for organisational change:

- Changes in the market-place
- New technology and ways of working
- New product development
- Acquisition of another organisation
- Change of strategic direction.

Examples of *Restraining Forces* against organisational change:

- Cost of change is prohibitive
- Trade union opposition
- Risk of adverse publicity
- Loss of employee goodwill and morale
- Lack of familiarity with new ways of working.

When the driving forces and restraining forces are balanced, there is 'equilibrium' and change does not occur. To make an organisational change effective, managers therefore need to introduce an imbalance. This can be done by adding or negating forces on either side.

The four main stages involved in using Force Field Analysis are:

1. Identifying all the driving forces and restraining forces
2. Quantifying the strength of each force to establish whether the net force is for or against change
3. Creating an imbalance in favour of the change, either by adding to the driving forces or mitigating against the restraining forces
4. Monitoring the impact of the change after it has occurred in order to ensure the benefits of change are maintained.

So what?

Force Field Analysis helps managers determine the appropriate action to take in order to support an organisational change.

The approach can be used to assess the forces in favour or against any management proposal that has been put forward.

Lewin advocated that the driving forces should not be increased simply to counteract opposition, as this could result in increased tension in those 'forced' to change.

Managers therefore need to consider some of the other tactics available to them. For example, Schlesinger and Kotter (1979) suggested that employee resistance could be overcome using education, participation, facilitation, negotiation, manipulation and/or coercion.

Procurement application

- Useful mapping tool for managing the implementation of procurement initiatives
- Helpful application for developments in the procurement function.

Limitations

Planning and evaluating the impact of organisational change is an imprecise art – not least of all because of the huge number of dynamics at play. Any model that therefore professes to predetermine employee responses to change is, at best, limited.

Although there is little to criticise the concept behind Force Field Analysis, there are several potential drawbacks in its application.

One of the key risks is whether the manager has successfully identified and assessed all of the driving forces and restraining forces. Should they have overlooked one of the forces, then the analysis is incomplete and could give the wrong answer.

Similarly, the process of quantification is also limited, as it is virtually impossible to predict and quantify the force of support or opposition to a proposed change.

The model therefore remains a useful managerial guide for assessing the impact of change. It has stood the test of time for the last 70+ years without replacement and therefore qualifies as one of procurement's most popular models.

Further reading

Lewin originally wrote about Force Field Analysis in:

Lewin, K. (1947). Frontiers in group dynamics. *Human Relations*, 1, 5–41.

You can read more about organisational change and Lewin's theories in:

Boddy, D. (2016). *Management: An Introduction.* 7th edition. Harlow: Pearson.

Associated models

- McKinsey 7S Framework (Model 48)
- Organisational Change (Model 54).

MODEL 52
LEAN VS. AGILE SUPPLY

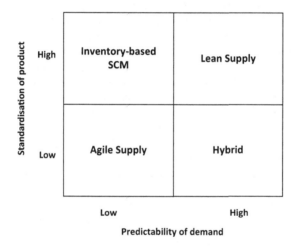

Figure 6.5   Lean vs. Agile Supply

Source: adapted from Christopher and Towill (2000).

Overview

During the late 1990s and early 2000s much airtime was given to the supply chain management debate. Some argued for 'lean supply' (and still do) whereas others claimed an 'agile supply chain' was more appropriate.

Martin Christopher and Denis Towill (2000) have written extensively on the subject in an attempt to draw the parallels and distinctions between these two different forms of supply chain management.

The model may not be conclusive for many procurement practitioners, but it certainly helps de-code some of the theoretical debate.

Elements

Lean supply – The principles of lean supply are based on those of lean production – the manufacturing philosophy of customer focus and efficiency of operation. In effect, the model suggests that where the demand for a standard product is predictable and certain then a lean supply chain will offer the best solution. This is supported with many empirical examples, such as that found in most automotive supply chains.

Agile supply – Agile supply, as the name suggests, is based on the quick response of a supply chain to new demands. These might be in the form of new product innovations or unpredictable order volumes. Agile supply chains tend to be very focused on short lead times and quick response to the customer. Typically, fashion retail supports this type of model.

Inventory-based SCM – Also referred to as 'top-up agile', the model suggests that where demand is unpredictable for standard products, the orders are most likely to be filled from existing stock solutions, inventory based management or potentially an agile supply option.

Hybrid – There have been a number of suggestions for this scenario in which the demand is unpredictable and the nature of the product is non-standard. This might take the form of a de-coupled 'postponement' strategy, where finished goods are stored in readiness to fulfil demand as it becomes known.

So what?

This is about how organisations manage their supply chains and the relationships with individual vendors.

Where stable conditions prevail, there is the opportunity to engage in lean supply – and with it, all the associated tools and techniques, such as total quality, six sigma, business process reengineering and so on. Typically, long-term collaborative relationships will be required where the focus is upon efficiency maximisation.

Where unstable conditions prevail, an agile supply chain is required. The focus needs to be on responsiveness, innovation and design. The philosophy is different, but the strong base of collaborative supply relationships is still a necessity.

Procurement application

- Helps define the strategic contribution of the supply chain
- Aligns supply-based activities with the operational goals and objectives of the organisation
- Defines the parameters of successful buyer–supplier relationships.

Limitations

The model helps to make the distinction between lean and agile supply chains at a theoretical level. However, this is where the practical use of the model stops – it does not inform the practitioner what they should be doing. In many ways it has a helpful but somewhat limited application.

Further reading

You can read more about the distinctions between lean and agile supply chains in:

Christopher, M. (2005). *Logistics and Supply Chain Management*. 3rd edition. Harlow: FT Prentice Hall.

Associated models

- Strategy Development (PCA Model) (Model 12)
- Relationship Continuum (Model 21)
- Kraljic Matrix (Model 22)
- Early Supplier Involvement (Model 27).

MODEL 53

INNOVATION DIFFUSION MATRIX

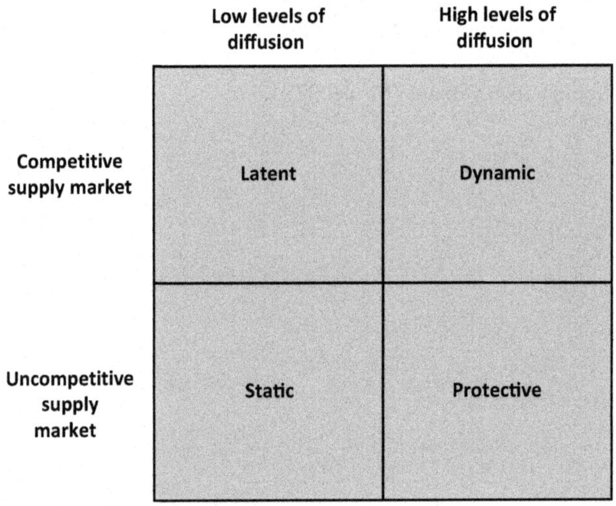

Figure 6.6 Innovation Diffusion Matrix

Overview

Innovation diffusion relates to the speed and extent to which a supplier's market is likely to adopt new products, services and/or processes. This depends on several factors, including aspects of culture, competition, profitability, capital investment, protectionism and regulation. Typically it can be measured by the number of product launches and/or rate of version control in any given market.

This model helps buyers to assess the market and identify the most appropriate course of action to achieve supplier innovation.

Elements

The Innovation Diffusion Matrix requires the buyer to assess the relative strength of competitive forces within the supply market, with that of innovation diffusion. There are four competitive approaches available to the buyer depending on the type of market:

Latent markets – The diffusion of innovation in the supply market is relatively low, despite the high levels of competition. This is typical of traditional markets, such as construction or heavy manufacturing, where the buyer needs to use ***competitive leverage*** to drive innovation and product development.

Dynamic markets – High levels of competition in the supply market go hand-in-hand with high levels of diffusion. This is typical of many fast-moving consumer-led markets, such as electronics and/or software, where the buyer needs to ***control development*** in order to create a sustained competitive position.

Static markets – Low levels of diffusion and competition within the market are typical of monopolistic and protected markets. Buyers need to exert ***aggregated bargaining power*** or the ***threat of substitutes*** to create any degree of innovation or development.

Protective markets – This refers to supply markets where there is relatively low competition and yet a high degree of innovation. These markets tend to be 'protective' towards innovation and development, often utilising their intellectual property to release innovation in a controlled manner so as to maintain a dominant position in the market. Where the buyer has little or no leverage, it can either use the ***threat of substitutes*** or simply ***accept the supply market offerings***.

So what?

Procurement is regularly required to work with suppliers to improve existing products and services. This model helps buyers to analyse the supply market that they are sourcing from and to formulate competitive strategies for getting improvements in product functionality, service, quality and/or cost.

Procurement application

- Supplier development – working with suppliers to improve existing products and services
- Supplier relationship management – managing complex or strategic suppliers so as to improve performance or enhance existing offerings
- New product development – harnessing the capabilities in the supply market to assist with the creation and launch of new products and services.

Limitations

Competition and diffusion are both subjective attributes, with no specific measures – they end up being relative and qualitative. Users therefore need to undertake a full supply market analysis before utilising the model.

Although the model is useful for helping buyers to think through the competitive strategy that they need to undertake, the outputs are fairly generalised. Further work is required to determine the strategy that is applicable in each specific circumstance.

Further reading

You can read more about innovation diffusion theory in:

Lynch, R. (2018). *Strategic Management*. 8th edition. Harlow: Pearson.

Associated models

- Competition Analysis (Model 15)
- SWOT Analysis (Model 17)
- PESTLE (Model 18)
- Early Supplier Involvement (Model 27).

MODEL 54
ORGANISATIONAL CHANGE

Scope of change

	Realignment	Transformation
Incremental	ADAPTATION	EVOLUTION
'Big Bang'	RECONSTRUCTION	REVOLUTION

Nature of change

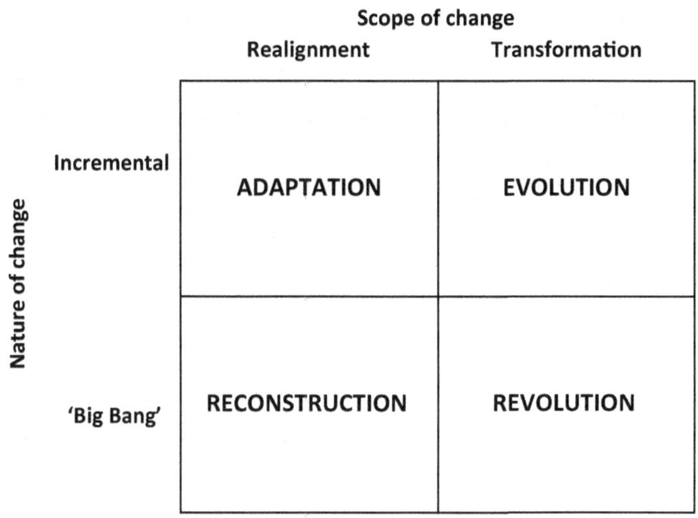

Figure 6.7 Organisational Change

Source: adapted from Balogun and Hope Hailey (1999).

Overview

There are many change models in existence, however few that deal with how it may be classified organisationally.

Professors Julia Balogun and Veronica Hope Hailey (1999) jointly published their model which is applied primarily in the context of the firm, and classification is based upon the speed and level of transformation required.

Elements

The 'Speed' variable ranges from big bang (all at once over a short space of time) to step by step (slow/incremental), whilst the extent of the 'Change' can be viewed as either transformational (outside of the existing business paradigm) or strategic realignment. Therefore, based upon these parameters organisational change can be identified as follows:

Evolution – This refers to transformational change implemented gradually through interrelated initiatives. It is likely to be proactive change initiated at a strategic level undertaken in anticipation of the need for future change. An example of this might be an organic growth strategy based on diversification.

Adaptation – This is change which is undertaken to realign the way in which the organisation operates, implemented in a series of steps such as a sustained advertising campaign.

Revolution – This is transformational change that occurs via simultaneous initiatives on many fronts; more likely to be forced and reactive because of the changing competitive conditions that the organisation is facing such as mergers and acquisitions.

Reconstruction – This refers to change undertaken to realign the way in which the organisation operates, with many initiatives implemented simultaneously; often forced and reactive because of a changing competitive context. For example, changing a purchasing function from a tactical to strategic orientation.

So what?

Change initiatives within the procurement function could include the implementation of a new Purchase-to-Pay system, switching key suppliers and realigning autonomous supply chain functions.

The beauty of this model is its simplicity. The matrix clearly shows how the variables of speed and type of change correlate in order to provide a classification mechanism, which can be easily interpreted and applied across a number of scenarios.

Procurement application

- Simple analysis tool which can aid the purchasing function classify types of change occurring within the function/organisationally
- Useful framework for discussing procurement initiatives with stakeholders
- Well recognised management tool that can be used in the strategic purchasing plan.

Limitations

There is a dearth of empirical research when it comes to change management within organisations, despite Balogun and Hope Hailey reporting that around 70% of all change programmes fail.

Academics contend that due to the constant state of flux that organisations find themselves in, they tend to have a reactive rather than a proactive change strategy, which therefore undermines several of the classifications within the Balogun and Hope Hailey framework.

Further reading

You can read more about Organisational Change and Balogun and Hope Hailey's theories in:

Balogun, J. and Hope Hailey, V. (1999). *Exploring Strategic Change*. 1st edition. Harlow: Prentice Hall.

Hope Hailey, V. and Balogun, J. (2002). Devising context sensitive approaches to change: the example of Glaxo Wellcome. *Long Range Planning*, 35(2), 153–178.

Balogun, J., Hope Hailey, V. and Gustafsson, S. (2016). *Exploring Strategic Change*. 4th Edition. Harlow: Pearson Education Limited.

Associated models

- McKinsey 7S Framework (Model 48)
- Force Field Analysis (Model 51).

BIBLIOGRAPHY AND SUGGESTED FURTHER READING

Adair, J. (1979). *Action-Centred Leadership*. London: Gower Publishing.

Ansoff, H.I. (1957). Strategies for diversification. *Harvard Business Review*, 35(5), 113–124.

Ansoff, H.I. (1984). *Implementing Strategic Management*. Englewood Cliffs, NJ: Prentice Hall International.

Baily, P., Farmer, D., Crocker, B., Jessop, D. and Jones, D. (2015). *Procurement Principles and Management*. 11th edition. Harlow: Pearson.

Balogun, J. and Hope Hailey, V. (1999). *Exploring Strategic Change*. 1st edition. Harlow: Prentice Hall.

Balogun, J. Hope Hailey, V. and Gustafsson, S. (2016). *Exploring Strategic Change*. 4th edition. Harlow: Pearson Education Limited.

Berrien, F.K. (1944). *Practical Psychology*. New York: Macmillan.

Blanchard, K., Carew, D. Pandarisi-Carew, E. (2004). *The One Minute Manager Builds High Performing Teams (The One Minute Manager)*. London: HarperCollins Publishers.

Blake, R.R., Mouton, J.S. and Bidwell, A.C. (1962). The Managerial Grid. *Advanced Management – Office Executive*, 1(9), 12–15.

Blake, R.R. and Mouton, J.S. (1964). *The Managerial Grid*. Houston, TX: Gulf Publishing.

Blake, R.R. and Mouton, J.S. (1985). *The Managerial Grid III: A New Look at the Classic That Has Boosted Productivity and Profits for Thousands of Corporations Worldwide*. Houston, TX: Gulf Publishing Co.

Boddy, D. (2016). *Management: An Introduction*. 7th edition. Harlow: Pearson.

Booth, C. (2010). *Strategic Procurement: Organizing Supplier and Supply Chains for Competitive Advantage*. London: Kogan Page.

Buchanan, D.A. and Huczynski, A.A. (2016). *Organizational Behaviour*. 9th edition. Harlow: Pearson.

Carter, R. (1995). The Seven Cs of effective supplier evaluation. *Purchasing and Supply Management*, April, 44–45.

Carter, R. and Kirby, S. (2006). *Practical Procurement*. Cambridge: Cambridge Academic.

Christopher, M. (2005). *Logistics and Supply Chain Management*. 3rd edition. Harlow: FT Prentice Hall.

Christopher, M. and Towill, D.R. (2000). Supply chain migration from lean and functional to agile and customised. *Supply Chain Management: An International Journal*, 5(4), 206–213.

Clegg, H. and Montgomery, S. (2005). Seven steps for sourcing information products. *Information Outlook*, 9(12).

Cordell, A. (2018). *The Negotiation Handbook*. 2nd edition. Oxon: Routledge.

Cordell, A. and Thompson, I. (2018). *The Category Management Handbook*. Oxon: Routledge.

Cox, A. (1996). Relational competence and strategic procurement management: towards an entrepreneurial and contractual theory of the firm. *European Journal of Purchasing & Supply Management*, 2(1), 57–70.

Cox, A. (1997). *Business Success*. Boston, MA: Earlsgate Press.

Cox, A. (2014). *Sourcing Portfolio Analysis*. Boston, MA: Earlsgate Press.

Cox, A., Ireland, P., Lonsdale, C., Sanderson, J. and Watson, G. (2002). *Supply Chains, Markets and Power: Mapping Buyer and Supplier Power Regimes*. London: Routledge.

Cox, A. and Thompson, I (1998). *Contracting for Business Success*. London: Thomas Telford.

Cummins, T., David, M. and Kawamoto, K. (2011). *Contract and Commercial Management: The Operational Guide*. Zaltbommel, The Netherlands: Van Haren Publishing.

Daft, R.L. and Lengel, R.H. (1998). *Fusion Leadership: Unlocking the Subtle Forces That Change People and Organisations*. San Francisco, CA: Berrett-Koehler Publishers Inc.

Deming, W.E. (1982). *Out of the Crisis*. Cambridge, MA: Massachusetts Institute of Technology, Center for Advanced Educational Services.

Emery, B. (2013). *Fundamentals of Contract and Commercial Management*. Zaltbommel, The Netherlands: Van Haren Publishing.

Fisher, R. and Ury, W.L. (1981). *Getting to Yes: Negotiating Agreement without Giving In*. Boston, MA: Houghton Mifflin.

Goldratt, E.M. (1990). *What Is This Thing Called Theory of Constraints?* Great Barrington, MA: North River Press Publishing Corporation.

Goldratt, E.M. (1997). *Critical Chain*. Great Barrington, MA: North River Press Publishing Corporation.

Greaver, M.F. (1999). *Strategic Outsourcing: A Structured Approach to Outsourcing Decisions and Initiatives*. New York: Amacom.

Greenhalgh, L. (2001). *Managing Strategic Relationships: The Key to Business Success*. New York: Simon and Schuster Adult Publishing Group.

Handy, C. (2000). *21 Ideas for Managers*. San Francisco, CA: Jossey-Bass.

Henderson, B.D. (1984). *The Logic of Business Strategy*. New York: Ballinger Publishing Co.

Hersey, P. (1984). *The Situational Leader*. Escondido, CA: Center for Leadership Studies.

Hersey, P. and Blanchard, K. (1974). So you want to know your leadership style? *Training and Development Journal*, February.

Hersey, P., Blanchard, K. and Natemeyer, W.E. (1979). Situational leadership, perception and the impact of power. *Group and Organizational Studies*, December, 418–428.

Hersey, P. Blanchard, K. and Johnson, D.E. (2001). *Management of Organizational Behavior: Leading Human Resources*. 8th edition. Harlow: FT Prentice Hall.

Hersey, P. Blanchard, K. ad Johnson, D.E. (2013). *Management of Organizational Behavior: Leading Human Resources*. 10th edition. Harlow: FT Prentice Hall.

Hope Hailey, V. and Balogun, J. (2002). Devising context sensitive approaches to change: the example of Glaxo Wellcome. *Long Range Planning*, 35(2), 153–178.

Ishikawa, K. (1968). *Guide to Quality Control*. Tokyo: JUSE.

Ishikawa, K. (2012). *Introduction to Quality Control*. New York: Springer.

Johnson, G. (1987). *Strategic Change and the Management Process (Corporate Strategy, Organization & Change)*. Hoboken, NJ: Wiley-Blackwell.

Johnson, G., Scholes, K. and Whittington, R. (2005). *Exploring Corporate Strategy Text and Cases*. 7th edition. Harlow: Pearson Education Limited.

Johnson, G., Whittington, R., Scholes, K., Angwin, D. and Regner, P. (2017). *Exploring Strategy: Text and Cases*. 11th edition. Harlow: Pearson.

Johnson, V.E., de Villiers, J.G. and Seymour, H.N. (2005). Agreement without understanding? The case of third person singular /s/. *First Language*, 25(3), 317–330.

Kaplan, R.S. and Norton, D.P. (1996). *The Balanced Scorecard: Translating Strategy into Action*. HBS Press.

Kraljic, P. (1983). Purchasing must become supply management. *Harvard Business Review*, 61(5), September–October, 109–117.

Lax, D.A. and Sebenius, J.K. (1986). *The Manager as Negotiator: Bargaining for Cooperation and Competitive Gain*. New York: The Free Press.

Levitt, T. (1965). *Exploit the Product Life Cycle*. Boston, MA: Graduate School of Business Administration Harvard University.

Lewicki, R.J., Saunders, D. and Barry, B. (2009). *Negotiation*. 6th edition. Burr Ridge, IL: McGraw Hill.

Lewin, K. (1947). Frontiers in group dynamics. *Human Relations*, 1, 5–41.

Lewin, K., Lippit, R. and White, R.K. (1939). Patterns of aggressive behavior in experimentally created social climates. *Journal of Social Psychology*, 10, 271–301.

Lonsdale, C. and Cox, A. (1998). *Outsourcing: A Business Guide to Risk Management Tools and Techniques*. Boston, UK: Earlsgate Press.

Luft, J. and Ingham, H. (1955). The Johari Window: a graphic model of interpersonal awareness. *Proceedings of the Western Training Lboratory in Group Development*. Los Angeles, CA: UCLA.

Lynch, R. (2018). *Strategic Management*. 8th edition. Harlow: Pearson.

Lysons, K. and Farrington, B. (2012). *Purchasing & Supply Chain Management*. 8th edition. Harlow: FT Prentice Hall.

Maslow, A.H. (1943). A theory of human motivation. *Psychological Review*, 50(4), 370–396.

Maslow, A.H., Stephens, D.C. and Heil, G. (1998). *Maslow on Management*. New York: John Wiley & Sons Inc.

Maylor, H. (2010). *Project Management*. 4th edition. Harlow: FT Prentice Hall.

McGregor, D. (1957). The human side of enterprise, in adventure in thought and action. *Proceedings of the Fifth Anniversary Convocation of the MIT School of Industrial Management*, June 1957, pp. 23–30; also *The Management Review*, 46(11), 22–28.

McGregor, D. (1960). *Human Side of Enterprise*. New York: McGraw-Hill.

Mendelow, A. (1991). *Proceedings of the Second International Conference on Information Systems*. Cambridge, MA: SMIS.

Mullins, L. (2016). *Management and Organisational Behaviour*. 11th edition. Harlow: Pearson.

Neely, A., Adams, C. and Kennerley, M. (2002). *The Performance Prism: The Scorecard for Measuring and Managing Business Success*. Harlow: Pearson.

O'Brien, J. (2017). *The Buyer's Toolkit: An Easy-to-use Approach for Effective Buying*. London: Kogan Page.

Peters, T. and Waterman, R. (1982). *In Search of Excellence: Lessons from America's Best-Run Companies*. New York: Harper & Row Publishers Inc.

Porter, M.E. (1980). *Competitive Strategy: Techniques for Analysing Industries & Competitors*. New York: The Free Press.

Porter, M.E. (1985). *Competitive Advantage: Creating and Sustaining Superior Performance*. New York: The Free Press.

Rackham, N. (1995). *SPIN® Selling*. Aldershot, UK: Gower.

Reynolds, A. (2003). *Emotional Intelligence and Negotiation*. Hampshire: Tommo Press.

Ruble, T.L. and THOMAS, K.W. (1976). Support for a two-dimensional model for conflict behaviour. *Organizational Behaviour and Human Performance*, 16, 143–155.

Sadgrove, K. (2007). *The Complete Guide to Business Risk Management*. 2nd edition. Aldershot, UK: Gower.

Schlesinger, L.A. and Kotter, J.P. (1979). Choosing strategies for change. *Harvard Business Review*, 57(2).

Schuh, C., Raudabaugh, J., Kromoser, R., Strohmer, M. and Triplat, A. (2012). *The Purchasing Chessboard*. 2nd edition. London: Springer Science and Business Media.

Shannon, C. (1948). A mathematical theory of communication. *Bell System Technical Journal*, 27 (July and October), 379–423, 623–656.

Slack, N., Brandon-Jones, A. and Johnston, R. (2016). *Operations Management*. 8th edition. Harlow: Pearson.

Steele, P.T. and Court, B.H. (1996). *Profitable Purchasing Strategies*. Singapore: McGraw-Hill.

Smith, W.P. (1987). Conflict and negotiation: trends and emerging issues. *Journal of Applied Social Psychology*, 17(7), 631–677.

Tannenbaum, R. and Schmidt, W.H. (1973). How to choose a leadership pattern. *Harvard Business Review*, May/June.

Tuckman, B. (1965). Developmental sequence in small groups. *Psychological Bulletin*, 63, 384–399.

Tuckman, B.W. and Jensen, M.A.C. (1977). Stages of a small-group development revisited. *Group & Organization Studies*, 2, 419–427.

Van Weele, A.J. and Rozemeijer, F. (1996). Revolution in purchasing: building competitive power through pro-active purchasing. *European Journal of Purchasing & Supply Management*, 2(4), 153–163.

Vitasek, K. (2011). *The Vested Outsourcing Manual: A Guide for Creating Successful Business and Outsourcing Agreements*. New York: Palgrave Macmillan.

Wynstra, F. and Ten Pierick, E. (2000). Management of supplier involvement in new product development. *European Journal of Purchasing and Supply Management*, 6, 49–57.

INDEX

Printed in the United States
by Baker & Taylor Publisher Services